Michael J. Phillips
Publisher & Editor-in-Chief

Terry Brisco	Executive Editor
Wendy Mellaerts	Production Director
Ciaran Oliver	Photographic Director
Sylvia Phillips	Editorial Director
James Graham	Marketing Manager
Patrick Broderick	Aerial Photography
Courtney Platt	Aerial Photography
David Wolfe	Aerial Photography
Dr. Philip Pedley	Special Advisor
Bert Leemans	Printing Director
Tony Barlow	Financial Director
Greet Timmermans	Graphics Director
Debbie Phillips	Text Editor
Wilfried Smets	Art Director
Henri Van de Weyer	Imaging Editor
Rudi Korthout	Colour Control Director
David Phillips	Public Relations Director
Anne Belle	Administration Manager

Publisher Review Publishing Company Ltd, St. Helier, Jersey, Channel Islands

Printer Agora Printing N.V., Geel, Belgium

Production Review Publishing Company Ltd, St. Helier, Jersey, Channel Islands

Photography Miguel Escalante, Landon Sterling, Patrick Gorham

We would like to thank the following for their helpful collaboration:
Hon. McKeeva Bush, Jennifer Dilbert, Charles Parchment, Dax Basdeo, Ted Bravakis, Pilar Bush, Natalie Coleman, Roger Craig, Eduardo D'Angelo P. De Silva, Virginia Dixon, Anita Ebanks, Jo Gammage, Kathy Jackson, David Legge, Christian Lennon, Don McDougall, Franz Manderson, Chris Mann, Angela Miller, Henry Muttoo, Cornelia Olivier, Rare Book Department of the Free Library of Philadelphia, Eloise Reid, Frank Roulstone, Terri Scott, Claudette Upton. Cayman Islands maps (pages 6-7) courtesy of Avis/Cico Rent-A-Car System Ltd.

Head Office Review Publishing Company Ltd, Nautilus House, La Cour des Casernes, St.Helier, Jersey JE1 3NH, Channel Islands
Fax: +44 (0)1534 760007

DISTRIBUTION

Cayman Islands	Hobbies And Books Ltd. P.O. Box 900 GT, Piccadilly Centre, Elgin Avenue, Grand Cayman, Cayman Islands Tel: (+1) 345 949 0707 • Fax: (+1) 345 949 7165
Jersey	Channel Island Publishing, Unit 3B, Barrette Commercial Centre, La Route Du Mont Mado, St. John, Jersey JE3 4DS, Channel Islands Tel: +44 (0)1534 860806 • Fax: +44 (0)1534 860811
Guernsey	Burbridge Limited, Publications Division, Les Câches, St. Martin, Guernsey 9Y4 6PH, Channel Islands Tel: +44 (0)1481 235656 • Fax: +44 (0)1481 234562
Great Britain	Review Publishing Company Ltd, Unit 1, Leigh Green Industrial Estate, Appledore Road, Tenterden, Kent TN30 7DF, United Kingdom. Fax: +44 (0)1580 765 056
Belgium	Altera Diffusion, Rue Emile Féron 168, B-1060 Brussels, Belgium Tel: +32 (0)2 543 06 00 • Fax: +32 (0)2 543 06 09
Luxembourg	Librairie Ernster, 27 rue du Fossé, L-1536 Luxembourg Tel: +352 (0)22 50 77-1 • Fax: +352 (0)22 50 73
The Netherlands	Betapress B.V., Burg Krollaan 14, NL-5126PT Gilze, The Netherlands Tel: +31 (0)161 457800 • Fax:+31 (0)161 457666
North America	Revista Auge de Mexico, Ave Presidente Masaryk 101, Col Polanco, 11560 Mexico DF, Mexico Tel: +52 (0)55 2810 • Fax: +52 (0)03 4061
All other countries	Review Publishing Company Ltd, Avenue Prince Charles 4, B-1410 Waterloo, Belgium Tel: +32 (0)2 353 18 80 • Fax: +32 (0)2 687 29 42

Contents

Introduction	6
History	8
Today	12
Financial Centre	16
George Town	22
Financial Regulation	28
Heroes Square	34
Banking	38
National Museum	44
National Gallery	46
Funds	48
Trusts	60
Legal System	68
Captive Insurance	76
Economy	82
Stock Exchange	90
Port of George Town	96
Tourism	104
Carnival	106
Seven Mile Beach	110
Real Estate	114
District of West Bay	124
Turtle Farm	128
Watersports	138
North Sound	140
Stingray City	141
Agriculture	142
Gastronomy	144
District of Bodden Town	148
Pedro St. James	152
District of North Side	154
Mastic Trail	159
Underwater World	160
District of East End	164
Botanic Park	166
Birds	170
Art and Culture	172
Weddings	175
Cayman Brac	176
Little Cayman	180
Health Care	184
Education	186
People	188
Index	189

www.internationalreview.com
e-mail: international.review@skynet.be

Cover Photograph
Courtney Platt

ISBN 0-9535447-8-8

Destination Cayman Islands

Editorial

As an international publisher of some 38 years' standing, it is my privilege to dedicate this special edition to the Cayman Islands. Having spent some six months living and working in Grand Cayman and the 'Sister Islands', I gained an appreciation of the people, their culture and the local way of life. What struck me, above all, was the optimism, courtesy and genuine friendliness of the Caymanian people – attributes that are so sadly lacking in much of our modern world.

Over the last few decades, this small group of islands has succeeded in becoming the world's leading offshore financial centre and its fifth-largest banking centre – largely thanks to the ambition, drive and expertise of Caymanians and their professional colleagues from around the world. Residents here, it is worth noting, enjoy a safe environment as well as the highest standard of living in the Caribbean.

Tourism too plays a major role in this economic success story. As I quickly discovered, Cayman has a near-perfect climate, is blessed with beautiful beaches, offers a selection of first-class accommodation and some of the region's finest restaurants, as well as a wide choice of sport and recreational activities. Couple these advantages with a surprisingly diverse and scenic landscape and an enlightened attitude to environmental protection – including conservation areas for some unique flora and fauna – and it is not hard to see why thousands of visitors return here time and time again.

I have also been impressed by the concerted effort made by the Government and private agencies to address and meet the special needs of each and every district in Grand Cayman as well as those of Cayman Brac and Little Cayman. This has entailed preserving cherished traditional values and practices, while ensuring the continued development of these areas.

These traditional values, not to mention a genuine sense of fun, are best experienced in Cayman's numerous festivals. Throughout the year, events such as Cayfest, Batabano Carnival and Pirates Week provide an opportunity for everyone to celebrate local art, music and culture and to engage with some memorable moments from the Islands' colourful maritime past.

In this book, we aim to provide an overview of the many and varied aspects of life today in the Cayman Islands. On behalf of my whole team, I would like to thank all those who have gone out of their way to help us in so many ways with the preparation of this special edition. To all of you, may I say a sincere thank you for your warm and friendly welcome. And to all those eager to learn more about this intriguing group of islands, I wish you happy reading!

Michael J. Phillips
Publisher & Editor-in-Chief

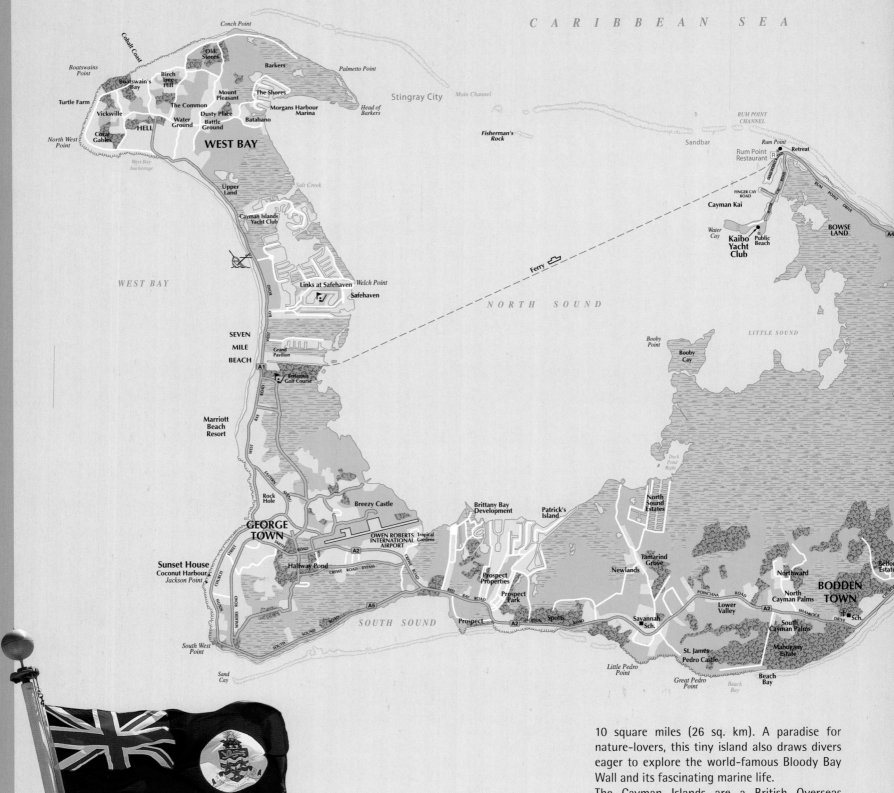

Introduction

The Cayman Islands are located in the western Caribbean, some 480 miles (770 km) south of Miami, 180 miles (290 km) north-west of Jamaica and 150 miles (240 km) south of Cuba. The total landmass of the three islands – Grand Cayman, Little Cayman and Cayman Brac – is 100 square miles (259 sq. km).

Grand Cayman is by far the largest of the trio. It is some 22 miles long (35.5 km), has an average width of four miles (6.5 km) and covers a total area of some 78 square miles (202 sq. km). The island is home to the vast majority of Cayman's total population of around 40,000. George Town,

the nation's capital and financial centre, is located on the west coast. The island is divided into five districts, namely George Town, West Bay, Bodden Town, East End and North Side.

One of the two 'Sister Islands', Cayman Brac lies some 89 miles (143 km) north-east of Grand Cayman and occupies 14 square miles (36.2 sq. km). This tranquil island with a population of around 1,800 features a spectacular limestone bluff rising to 140 feet (43 m) and is home to almost 200 species of bird. Its nearby neighbour, Little Cayman, has a resident population of around 115 and a surface area of approximately

10 square miles (26 sq. km). A paradise for nature-lovers, this tiny island also draws divers eager to explore the world-famous Bloody Bay Wall and its fascinating marine life.

The Cayman Islands are a British Overseas Territory, have their own Legislative Assembly and are largely self-governed. They were formerly a dependency of and administered by Jamaica but were given their own constitution in 1959. When Jamaica became independent from the UK in 1962, the Cayman Islands elected to become a British Crown Colony. The Governor is appointed by the Crown and the present Constitution provides for a legislative assembly of 15 elected members. General elections are held every four years. There is an eight-person cabinet, five of whom are appointed from and by the elected Assembly; the other three are appointed by the Governor. The legal system is based on the British system and complemented by local legislation. The local currency is the Cayman Islands dollar (CI$). However the US dollar is also widely used and trades at a rate of CI$0.80 to US$1.00.

The country enjoys a very pleasant climate all year round, with temperatures rarely dipping below 70°F (21°C) or rising above 90°F (32°C). The coolest season is from November to April.

Grand Cayman

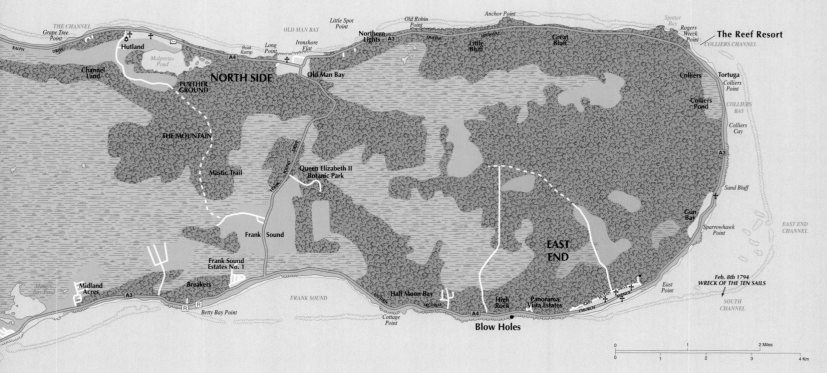

Caymanians are renowned for their friendliness and are a devout, church-going people. They are proud of their multiracial and multicultural origins. Around one in four are European, mainly descended from British settlers, a further quarter are of African descent, and the rest claim mixed ancestry. The official language is English, though Spanish is also spoken.

Until World War Two, most Caymanians made their living from turtling and seafaring. Today the country is a thriving international finance centre, home to the world's leading banks, financial service providers, and law and accounting firms. This successful industry, the mainstay of the economy, dates back to the passing of the first banking and trust laws in 1966.

Tourism is also a vital sector, thanks in large measure to the Islands' excellent weather, wide choice of accommodation, fine restaurants, glorious beaches, coral reefs and crystal-clear seas – home to some of the world's best diving spots. Duty-free shopping is another attraction for the thousands of tourists who arrive by air or on luxury cruise ships.

Cayman's three national symbols – the Silver Thatch Palm, the Grand Cayman Parrot and the Wild Banana Orchid – are as diverse as the Islands themselves.

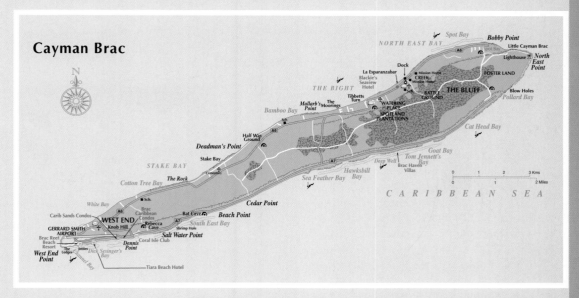

Cayman Brac

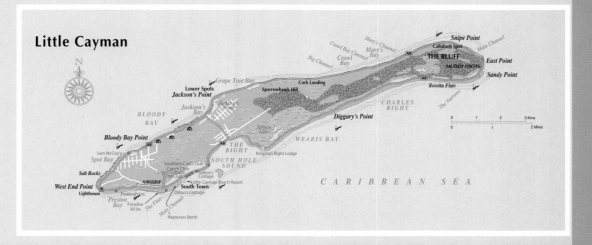

Little Cayman

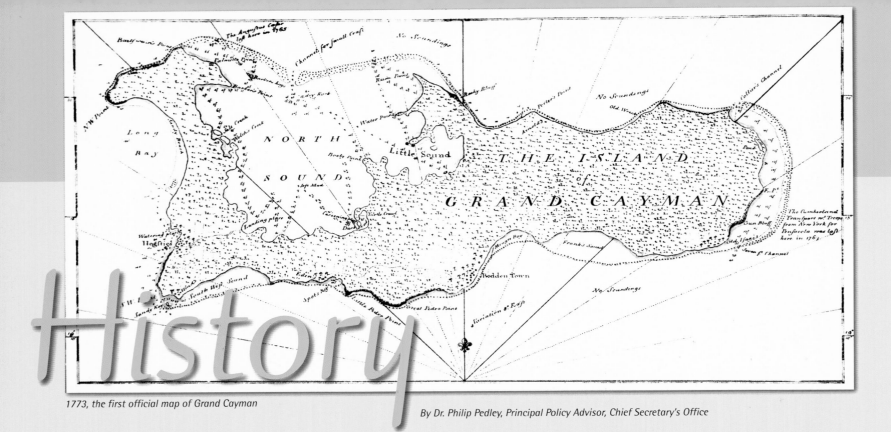

History

1773, the first official map of Grand Cayman

By Dr. Philip Pedley, Principal Policy Advisor, Chief Secretary's Office

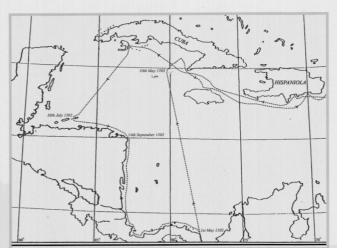

The final voyage of Columbus, 1502-1504

The discovery of Cayman over the last 40 years as a tourist destination and financial centre has sometimes fostered the view that before modern development these three islands were isolated, unknown specks of land in the expanse of the Western Caribbean. In fact, this is a myth of recent origin.

From 1500 onwards, throughout the age of sail, the Cayman Islands were navigational landmarks known to countless sailors from Spain, England, France and Holland, as early maps and logs of the Caribbean reveal. Until the coming of the steamship, the standard route for ships returning to Europe from the Western Caribbean was to sail west in order to travel east. The prevailing north-east winds and currents made it difficult to beat a passage between what is now Haiti and Cuba. It was easier and sometimes quicker to sail westwards around the tip of Cuba, pick up the wind on the ship's port beam, and head for the Atlantic. A schooner sailing west from Jamaica, for example, could well have set a lookout for Cayman Brac, whose sheer bluff – rising to 140 feet – might be seen ten miles away.

The presence of turtle also proved a powerful magnet for early mariners. These large animals were tasty and highly valued as a source of fresh meat. For almost 300 years, turtle's abundance on Cayman's beaches and in her waters attracted vessels from every nation caught up in the theatre of exploration, war and commerce into which Europe had transformed the Caribbean.

The first European to sight the Cayman Islands was probably Columbus, in 1503. The distinction of recording this event in fact belongs to his 14-year-old son, Ferdinand, who entered the following note in the log: "Wednesday May 10th, we sighted

Slaves logging near Bodden Town

Sir Francis Drake's fleet visits Grand Cayman, 1586

two very small low islands full of turtles (as was all the sea thereabout, so that it seemed to be full of little rocks); that is why these islands were called Las Tortugas".

This was Columbus's fourth and final voyage to the West Indies. His battered fleet, reduced from four vessels to two, both leaking badly, was limping homeward. Columbus himself must have been bitterly disappointed that all his efforts to reach India via a sea passage through Central America had failed. The islands he sighted that day were Cayman Brac and Little Cayman. It is sobering to reflect that when he died three years later, Columbus remained convinced that these two islands, like Cuba, were actually islands off the coast of Asia. No archaeological evidence of any pre-Columbian settlements has been found in Cayman, and the two Sister Islands Columbus described, as well as Grand Cayman, were almost certainly uninhabited.

For the next 200 years the Cayman Islands were known to thousands of explorers, sailors and adventurers, both for their fierce crocodiles – the 'caimanos' after which the islands were subsequently named – and for their turtles, prized as a provision that could be transported live on their backs for long periods or else salted for preservation. An early English description of Jamaica from 1662 reveals how important turtle was as a commodity. Under the heading 'Fish', the author notes that the most sought-after item was turtle and concludes: "to leeward of Port Negril lie the islands of Camanas, whither resort in May, June and July, all the men of war and merchant ships from the Caribbee Islands to victual and load with this fish, it being found and reputed to be the wholesomest and best provision in all the Indies".

Though Cayman was renowned for turtle, it was lumber, particularly mahogany, that first drew people to settle in any numbers there. As early as 1700, small-scale loggers and planters began to migrate from

Jamaica to Grand Cayman. For the next 60 years or so their numbers remained low – probably less than 200, including slaves. Passing ships record fascinating glimpses of this early Caymanian community. HMS Alarm, for example, provides this snapshot from 1764: "Here is 16 families in different parts that subsists in fishing and cutting mahogany. Small vessels from Jamaica brings them necessaries and carry off their produce. They have no civil or military officer among them nor do they appear to have any occasion for any, all living at peace with one another".

Cotton was introduced to the island about this time, eventually replacing lumber as the main export. Unlike Jamaica or Barbados, Cayman never had sugar plantations, but its cotton industry was producing about thirty tons annually by 1800. With the introduction of cotton, the demand grew for labour – and so for slaves. By 1802, when the Governor of Jamaica sent an official named Edward Corbet to report on

The proclamation freeing the slaves, 3 May 1835

Former slaves entertaining themselves

Cayman, the population had reached 933. All were living on Grand Cayman and slightly more than half were slaves. The population doubled during the next generation, reaching about 2,000 in 1834, the year slavery was abolished.

The 1830s proved to be an important decade. With the population growing and spreading into the districts and slave emancipation a near-certainty, there was a desire to strengthen government. In the early days, local magistrates appointed by Jamaica had tried to apply Jamaican law to Cayman. This proved impractical and in time the magistrates began to meet with other 'leading inhabitants' so as to fashion laws suitable for Cayman. On 5 December 1831, at a landmark meeting at Pedro St. James, this group decided to create the first elected legislature. Elections were held five days later. Unrecognised by Jamaica or Great Britain, the new assembly passed 'local laws' for the next 30 years. Its existence and legislation were finally sanctioned under a British Act of Parliament in 1863 that formally made Cayman a dependency of Jamaica. This arrangement continued for almost a century

until the constitutional link with Jamaica ended and Cayman became a Crown Colony.

Daily life between 1700 and 1900 was shaped by the islands' isolation and size. Cayman boasted few natural resources, but those available proved quite sufficient for a small population. If there were no large tracts of fertile soil, this scarcity hid a blessing: it failed to attract powerful landowners bent on creating commercial sugar plantations. Instead, each family worked the land and the sea to meet its needs. These factors nurtured a people who were hardy, independent and resourceful. From the 1780s onwards they were constructing schooners from local timber, trading with Jamaica and Central America, and catching turtles weighing hundreds of pounds from the waters off the Sister Islands and Grand Cayman. When local supplies of turtle dwindled, new sources were found, first off the coast of Cuba and then in the Nicaraguan cays. Shipbuilding and turtling skills were matched by expert seamanship. For many years, until well into the 20th century, Caymanian seamen could sail by dead reckoning for hundreds of miles in any

Turtle and "cayman", as seen by Drake's fleet

Pedro St. James: meeting to create an elected legislature in 1831

Surveying the land in the spirit of the early settlers

Rural Grand Cayman in 1906

direction in the Western Caribbean.

Life on land was simple and changed slowly. Houses were modest and constructed of 'wattle and daub', local wood and thatch. Cooking took place on a home-made 'caboose' housed in an outside 'cook-room'. The staple foods were fish and turtle, 'ground provisions' such as yams and sweet potatoes, and a wide variety of fruit. Beef was a rarity and mutton unknown. Roads were narrow and rough. Transport might be on foot or by donkey, horse or cart, but people also travelled from one district to another by canoe or sailing vessel. Clothing was plain, sometimes made from osnaburg linen or a rougher crocus cloth. Women played an important role in the emerging society, as witnessed by their presence as heads of families in the 1802 census. "The women are numerous," commented George Gauld, the Royal Navy hydrographer who drew the first official map of Grand Cayman in 1773, "and those that are natives of the island have a modesty in their dress and a decency in their behaviour not always to be met with between the tropics."

Caymanians, Gauld added, "were very desirous of having a clergyman and a surgeon to reside among them." Yet 60 years were to pass before the first trained ministers arrived in the 1830s, and a further 60 years before the wish for a resident doctor was fulfilled in the 1890s. Church and religious life were major forces shaping traditional Caymanian society. The pulpit was revered,

and ministers and churchmen established the first schools. In the 1840s Presbyterians took over the work begun in the previous decade by Anglicans and Methodists. For many years, Presbyterians formed the de facto established church on Grand Cayman.

Turtle being brought ashore in the North Sound

The Sister Islands were permanently settled from the 1830s, but were rarely visited by a minister until the mid-1880s, when Baptist missionaries from Jamaica pioneered six churches on Cayman Brac and Little Cayman. By 1900, Caymanians on the Sister Islands were as ardently Baptist as their near neighbours on Grand Cayman were firmly Presbyterian.

At the dawn of the 20th century, everyday life was in some respects little different from what it had been 50 or even a hundred years before. But the new century was to bring undreamed-of changes. At first the transformation was marked by gradual improvements in housing and roads, public education and public buildings, and by stronger links to the outside world through the construction of motor vessels and a wireless station. Although World War I hardly affected daily life in Cayman, the 1920s and 1930s witnessed an ebb and flow of Caymanians migrating to and from the United States as the boom of the twenties turned into the Great Depression.

Outside influences had a much greater

The opening of the first wireless station, George Town, 1935

effect on Cayman during World War II, when many Caymanians served in the merchant marine or in the Trinidad Royal Naval Volunteer Reserve, and a US naval base operated in George Town. After the war, the stirrings of modern development could be felt throughout the Caribbean region. Cayman was no exception, witnessing the start of commercial air travel in the late 1940s and the construction of the first hotels, a modern airport and a hospital in the next decade.

The pace of modern development gradually accelerated during the 1960s and 1970s. The financial industry took shape in the mid-1960s, land registration was formalised in the decade that followed, and tourism continued to grow – partly as a result of opportunities in offshore finance and land development. The three legs of the modern Cayman economy – financial services, tourism and real estate – became firmly established. New schools, health facilities, roads, commercial links by air and sea, and the conquest of the mosquito were all part of the modern infrastructure needed to support this development. By the 1980s and

industry attracting about 20,000 visitors each year. Over the next three decades, however, the population increased five times to a little under 50,000, while the number of tourists multiplied one hundred times, from 20,000 to over two million. More than a hundred nationalities can be found amongst those who now live and work in the islands, and for the last decade or so a majority of the workforce has come from outside Cayman.

Patterns of work altered dramatically during the last century. Until well into the 1950s, Caymanians earned their living from the sea, as turtlers or as seamen employed on National Bulk Carriers or other major shipping lines. Others moved abroad to find work in Cuba, Panama, Jamaica or North America, often settling in these countries while retaining strong ties to their homeland. Meanwhile, Caymanians at home depended on remittances from their seamen, busied themselves in local craft industries such as the production of rope from thatch, or pursued a living as district merchants.

As new development gathered momentum, these patterns disappeared. Caymanians ceased to venture abroad and migrated home. They sought employment in the new hotels and banks or in the growing ranks of government, while the older craft industries declined. For younger Caymanians, the pace and rhythms of modern life are a world away from those which shaped their grandparents or even their parents.

PBM Mariner supplying the US Navy Base, 1943

Into this confident, cosmopolitan community on 11 September, 2004 came the visitation known simply as 'Ivan'. Although previous hurricanes had wreaked great destruction on the Cayman Islands – those of 1780 and 1876, for example, were probably as terrifying, and the infamous storm of 1932 killed 108 people from Cayman Brac – Hurricane Ivan commanded special attention because its forces were unleashed on a much larger population and on the full fruits of modern development. Miraculously, only two lives were lost.

Time alone will tell what the social, cultural and spiritual effects of this major disaster will be. The first year of recovery witnessed frenetic activity in reconstruction coupled with a strong willingness to reinvest in what were once known as 'The Islands Time Forgot'. That a community so severely damaged could hold free and fair elections only eight months after the disaster, with 79% of registered voters participating, was striking testimony to its robust and resilient spirit. For many Caymanians, Hurricane Ivan and its long aftermath provided ample opportunity to reflect on the things that sustained them during days of unprecedented trauma. No small part of that sustenance was a deep pride in their heritage and a strong sense of identity rooted in a unique past.

Traditional schoolhouse at Creek, Cayman Brac

1990s, the tide of change had turned into a flood. Cayman had achieved global recognition as a major financial centre, tourist destination and real estate market.

Population trends over the last hundred years underpin this story. Between 1900 and 1950 the population slowly grew from about 5,000 to 7,000. By 1970 it had reached 10,000, with the nascent tourist

Traditional boatbuilding in 1906

Smiley Connolly's school, George Town, in the early 1900s

Modern housing

Cayman today

By William S. Walker OBE,
Chairman, Caledonian Bank & Trust Limited

Just one hour by plane from Miami, some 180 miles (290 km) north-west of Jamaica and 150 miles (240 km) south of Cuba, the Cayman Islands are located in the north-west Caribbean. The three small islands – Grand Cayman, Cayman Brac and Little Cayman – have a combined population of around 40,000, yet they are today famed worldwide for their thriving financial and tourist industries.

A politically stable democracy, Cayman is constitutionally a British Overseas Territory, the modern term for what was previously known as a Colony. It has an elected Government of Caymanian ministers and the Governor is appointed by HM the Queen.

The Islands – whose capital is George Town – enjoy a large measure of self-government and a new constitution is currently being negotiated. This is expected to come into force in the near future and will undoubtedly consist of a substantial advance in self-government.

Under the present constitution, the number of election votes Caymanians have depends on the constituency in which they live. Constituencies with the larger populations, such as West Bay and George Town, offer their voters up to four votes each, which corresponds to four members of the Legislative Assembly. The other constituencies each have fewer representatives and so fewer votes. Residents of North Side and East End, for example, have only one vote. This unusual system has been a matter of vigorous discussion for some years. Constitutional advancement could well include a change to 'one man one vote'. Voters would no longer vote for a whole district but for a single member constituency. In all, there could be 17 single-member constituencies, and each voter would vote only once within their constituency, as in most other Commonwealth countries.

Like all British Overseas Territories, Cayman is not represented in the British Parliament, although the British Parliament can legislate for the Cayman Islands. However, this is most unusual and generally speaking all legislation is enacted by the Legislative Assembly. As with other citizens of UK

Keeping the Islands safe

Beautiful sandy beaches

The mobile-phone generation

'Rundown', a popular annual satirical revue

A sports-lover's paradise

Overseas Territories, Caymanians now have the right to British Citizenship in addition to being Caymanian.

The Islands' Governor, a British official, retains certain reserve powers, the main ones being Foreign Relations, Defence and Internal Security. He or she also has control of the Courts, the Prosecution Service and the Police, although the vast majority of Officers who run these services are normally Caymanians or from other Commonwealth countries rather than from the United Kingdom.

Caymanians speak English, are well educated and renowned for their friendliness. Their Government does not impose income or corporation tax, nor tax on capital gains, inheritance or gifts. The currency is the Cayman Islands dollar (CI$), although the US dollar is also widely used and trades at a fixed rate of CI$0.80 to US$1.00.

The Cayman Islands have a good road network and an international airport served by a number of major airlines, with direct links to the United States and Europe. George Town is also the world's fourth busiest port for cruise ships, which carry some two million passengers – most from North America – to the Cayman Islands every year. Many of these visitors make the most of the opportunity to purchase the Islands' duty-free goods.

The Islands have two daily newspapers and one weekly, a growing number of local radio stations and a number of local television stations. They also offer locals and visitors a wide range of artistic, leisure and sports activities, though they are probably best known for their spectacular diving and snorkelling sites.

A varied and vibrant press

13

A wide and varied choice of restaurants

financial centre in the world. Our banks hold more than US$1.1 trillion in assets and the country is regarded as a well-regulated jurisdiction.

Today Cayman is also the preferred jurisdiction for the incorporation of hedge and mutual funds and features among the world leaders in fund administration. Although the actual investment management is seldom carried out in Cayman, the administration including the share registry function is normally performed here and, in many cases, funds have directors who reside in Cayman. The financial industry survived Hurricane Ivan successfully and most financial institutions were back in business within a matter of days or at most a couple of weeks.

This combination of tourism and finance has produced the highest standard of living in the Caribbean and offers the ordinary resident of the Cayman Islands the opportunity to enjoy a superior lifestyle. The Islands also enjoy a generally low crime rate.

The topography of the three islands – which are limestone outcroppings, the peaks of a submarine mountain range –

Cayman today

The economy of the Cayman Islands depends on two major sectors: tourism and offshore finance. The natural beauty of this group of Caribbean islands, their excellent climate (the temperature rarely dips below 70°F or 21°C), fascinating wildlife, beautiful beaches and sophisticated infrastructure of fine hotels and a range of other accommodation go a long way to explaining why tourism is so successful here today. Notwithstanding the damage to many tourist facilities and vegetation on Grand Cayman in September 2004, following the passage of Hurricane Ivan, a national clean-up campaign has virtually restored the island to its pre-hurricane condition.

As for offshore finance, Cayman was one of the first Commonwealth islands in the Caribbean to enter this field and has enjoyed extraordinary success in it. Today the Cayman Islands are the fifth-largest

Caymanians love to party

High-quality health care is readily available

does not allow for a big agricultural industry. Marshlands or rocky land cover much of the islands, fertile areas are few and far between, and labour costs are high. Though the Government has given some support to local agriculture, this industry is today effectively limited to market gardening. Fortunately, as a result of the strong economy and the proximity of the United States, Caymanians are able to import food and consumer goods of a high quality.

There is virtually no unemployment in Cayman. However, there is some resistance from Caymanians to performing menial jobs. This situation results in the importation of low-wage foreign labour, which causes some social and housing problems.

The majority of the Government and private schools on Cayman are geared to academic studies. At the George Town campus, the University College offers vocational, professional and academic programmes. The Cayman Islands Law School, although small, has built up an excellent academic record and performed a very useful function in offering young Caymanians the opportunity to become lawyers without having to go abroad. The Law School is affiliated with the University of Liverpool in England: its exams are set and marked in Liverpool and graduates of the school obtain the Liverpool LLB. As a result, almost half of the lawyers on the island are Caymanians. Grand Cayman is also home to St. Matthew's University School of Medicine.

The Cayman Islands have astonished the world by their significant development over

The chamber of the Legislative Assembly, home of the Islands' parliament

Rural Grand Cayman

the last three or four decades and more recently surprised outsiders by their quick recovery from the effects of Hurricane Ivan. Many challenges still remain, but Caymanians are committed to continuing to plough their successful furrow long into the future.

An outstanding education system

Merchandise from around the world grace the shops of Cayman

15

The world's leading offshore financial centre

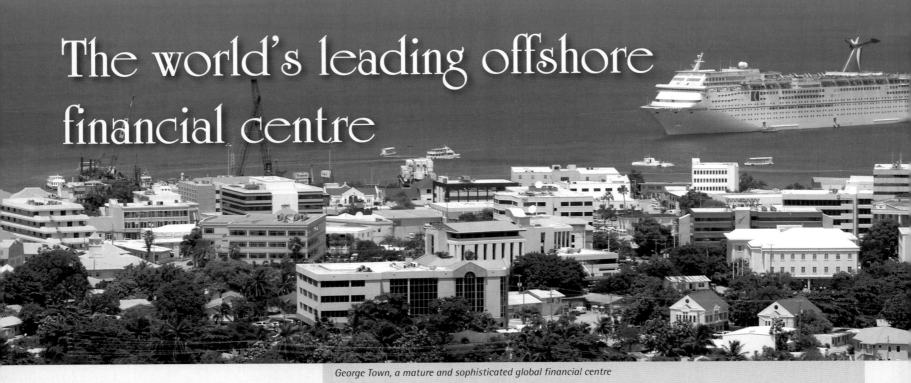

George Town, a mature and sophisticated global financial centre

By Stuart Dack, ACIB, MBA, President and CEO, Cayman National Corporation Ltd.

Readers will be forgiven if they are unable to locate the Cayman Islands on either a map or a globe. After all, they appear as just three tiny specks 480 miles south of Florida, surrounded by the Caribbean Sea.

And yet, if the scale of the map were drawn differently, based, say, on importance as an international financial centre as opposed to geographic square miles, the Cayman Islands would appear massive indeed. By some measures, including assets on deposit in Grand Cayman's 300-plus banks – more than US$1.0 trillion – the Cayman Islands would appear huge, ranking as the fifth-largest banking centre in the world. (On a per capita basis, Grand Cayman banks have close to US$25 million on deposit for each of the 40,000 residents living on the island.)

Collectively the Cayman Islands include three small islands – Grand Cayman, which is the residential and commercial centre of the country, and the sparsely populated 'Sister Islands' of Cayman Brac and Little Cayman which lie 80 miles to the north-east.

The depth and breadth of financial services – and the professional infrastructure that supports them – in the Cayman Islands are unsurpassed in other offshore jurisdictions. In addition to banking, Grand Cayman is a domicile of choice for offshore trusts – which in total assets comprise an even larger segment of Cayman's financial industry than banking – company formation and management, captive insurance, mutual funds, and growing airline and vessel registries. (The Cayman Islands flag flies on more 'super yachts' than any other jurisdiction's in the world.)

Not surprisingly the economy of the Cayman Islands is driven largely by two major industries, financial services and tourism, which developed in tandem and, to an extent, symbiotically.

In March 1982, the Honourable Financial Secretary Vassel Johnson presented a 'Cayman Islands Economic and Financial Review' to His Excellency The Governor Peter Lloyd. The Review said, in part, "The progress and economic stability of the Cayman Islands was indeed created by design and it did not all happen by sheer coincidence."

Major accounting, law and insurance management firms are represented in Grand Cayman

Indeed it did not. It is worthwhile – and instructive – to examine briefly how the Cayman Islands emerged from a small settlement into the thriving metropolis it has become today.

From the time Christopher Columbus discovered the Cayman Islands in 1503 until the meteoric growth began in recent decades, not much of historical significance took place on these islands.

The beginnings of change began to manifest themselves in the early 1960s when a small group of pioneers in the private sector forged a partnership with Government to create the beginnings of the financial industry we know today. Together they crafted legislation and regulation – effective but not punitive or onerous – that would form the foundation upon which the financial industry would be built. Some milestones in Cayman's financial history include:

• In 1953 the first bank in Grand Cayman, a branch of Barclays, opened in George Town, followed a decade later by The Royal Bank of Canada and Canadian Imperial Bank of Commerce (CIBC).

• In 1960 the first Companies Law was introduced, positioning the Cayman Islands as a domicile for company registrations.

• In 1966 the Banks and Trust Companies Law was enacted, setting the stage for future growth as a financial centre. This progressive legislation, local lore has it, was written in part in evenings on the kitchen table of a local attorney.

• In 1971 legislators adopted the Currency Law, and a Board of Commissioners was established to introduce Cayman's own currency. Today approximately CI$55 million is in circulation backed more than 100% by external reserves and linked in value to the US dollar.

• In 1979 the Insurance Law was introduced, enabling the captive insurance industry to gain a foothold – and eventually flourish – on the island.

• In 1993 the Cayman Islands enacted the Mutual Fund Law, which helped set the stage for the islands to attract the now-booming hedge fund industry. It is estimated that more than 80% of all the new funds in the world are being established in Grand Cayman.

• In 1997 the Cayman Islands Stock Exchange (CSX) came into being and has had rapid growth in its portfolio with more than 800 issues approved for listing.

• In 2003 the Cayman Islands passed comprehensive anti-terrorism legislation and adopted, as part of its domestic law, United Nations Security Council resolutions dealing with the financing of terrorism.

The great respect the Cayman Islands enjoy in the international financial community can be traced, in part, to the regulatory oversight provided by the Cayman Islands Monetary Authority (CIMA). This was established in 1996 to supervise Cayman's financial industry and to ensure compliance with applicable laws. (Prior to the formation of the Monetary Authority, financial supervision was carried out by the Financial Services Supervision Department and the Currency Board.)

Historically the Cayman Islands have met or exceeded international regulatory and supervisory standards. They have aligned themselves with the Basel Committee on Banking Supervision, the International Organisations of Securities Commissions (IOSCO), the Offshore Group of Banking Supervisors (OGBS), the Offshore Group of Insurance Supervisors (OGIS), the Caribbean Financial Action Task Force, and the Overseas Territories Regulators.

In place are bilateral mutual cooperation agreements, including the Mutual Legal Assistance Treaty with the United States, and various regulatory cooperation arrangements maintained by the Cayman Islands Monetary Authority. In 2001, the Cayman Islands and the U.S. enacted the Tax Information Exchange Agreement (TIEA). This enables the sharing of tax information between the two countries under certain defined circumstances.

After extensive consultation with local financial practitioners, the Cayman Islands Government agreed to implement the European Union Savings Tax Directive. This enables the exchange of information among EU member states, named third countries (Switzerland, San Marino, Monaco, Andorra and Liechtenstein) as well as associated and dependent territories

The world's fifth-largest banking centre

of EU member states.

In addition to enlightened legislation and regulatory supervision, the Cayman Islands as a financial centre have benefited greatly from a variety of factors that have contributed to their success. Some are man-made, some God-given, some merely serendipitous. These include:

• As a British Overseas Territory, the Cayman Islands enjoy a warm relationship with the Mother Country. Approximately every three years, the Queen (through the Foreign and Commonwealth Office) appoints a Governor who oversees the foreign affairs, security and good governance of the Cayman Islands.

• A legal system based on British Common Law with ultimate appeal to Britain's Privy Council.

• A stable democratically elected Government that looks after the local affairs of the country. Quadrennial elections are well contested and spirited but have always been peaceful.

• Tax neutrality and no direct personal, corporate or property taxes. (The Government receives its operating revenues principally from duties on imported goods, 'stamp duty' imposed on land and property transfers, and licence fees and permits required of businesses to operate.)

• A mature and sophisticated infrastructure that supports the financial community and its clients. All of the 'Big Four' accounting firms have major operations on the island, as do highly sophisticated law firms, company management and insurance management firms.

• A culturally conservative population that values such traditional traits as hard work, entrepreneurship and self-reliance.

On September 11, 2004, the Cayman Islands were put to their most severe historical test when Hurricane Ivan made landfall in Grand Cayman. It damaged or destroyed much of the island's infrastructure, resulting in structural and economic damage, as estimated in the United Nations ECLAC Report, of at least US$3.4 billion.

In the immediate aftermath of the storm, the financial community led the way both in its resilience and its assurance to the global financial community that Grand Cayman was indeed 'open for business.' Within days, electrical power and telecommunications had been restored to the downtown financial district, the airport had reopened, and the recovery had begun.

In the months following the storm, the same private sector/public sector cooperation that has served the Cayman Islands so well historically again came into play. Before, during, and after the storm, virtually all of the contingency, emergency and recovery operations were formulated and implemented with close consultation among Government, financial and tourism representatives.

The Cayman Islands financial community demonstrated not only its resilience but also its ability to conduct local and global transactions in the most trying of circumstances. The financial community had been put to the

Leading centre for company registration and management

ultimate test – and it passed convincingly.

Since the financial industry put down its roots 40 years ago in the Cayman Islands, its growth – both in quantity and in quality – has transformed these islands into the modern society they have become today. According to most experts and projections, this growth is likely to continue in the years ahead – and the islands are preparing for it.

Today approximately 6,400 hedge funds (out of the world's 8,000) are registered in Grand Cayman, and experts estimate that Cayman's registrations will double by 2010. Although the total numbers of banks and trust companies have contracted somewhat in recent years, due mainly to mergers and consolidations, the deposits in Cayman banks continue to swell, and that pattern is expected to continue.

As the financial industry in Grand Cayman has matured over the years, the private sector and the Government have made it clear that they are interested in doing business only with reputable, world-class investors and financial institutions. Investment opportunities abound for those who meet that profile. Others of dubious reputation need not apply and are not welcome in the Cayman Islands.

A recently released International Monetary Fund (IMF) report gives high grades to the Cayman Islands for the strength of their regulatory and anti money-laundering regimes. The report said, in part, "An extensive program of legislative, rule and guideline development has introduced an increasingly effective system of regulation, both formalising earlier practices and introducing enhanced procedures."

The report further stated, "The supervisory system benefits from a well-developed banking infrastructure with an internationally experienced and qualified workforce as well as experienced lawyers, accountants and auditors." It added that, "the overall compliance culture within Cayman is very strong, including the compliance culture related to AML [anti money-laundering] obligations."

Excellence in auditing

Ernst & Young, Cayman has a history of excellence that spans more than 30 years. As a dynamic and quality-driven audit firm, it has led the way in serving its clients as the financial landscape has evolved both locally and internationally.

While we might talk today of financial 'landscapes', the firm has grown out of a culture that for centuries was based around the sea and the sustenance it provided to the Caymanian people. The Islands' shipbuilders, sea captains, turtlers, fishermen and merchant sailors were renowned worldwide not only for their knowledge and skills in all things nautical but, perhaps even more important, for their traditional values of hard work, integrity, conservative beliefs and, above all, quality. Ernst & Young, Cayman still holds these traditional values of their forebears most dear. In fact, they are the defining culture of the firm. Appropriately, the motto for the firm is 'Quality in Everything We Do.'

Today the Cayman firm provides assurance and advisory business services to a variety of top-quality clients worldwide. It is affiliated with, and has access to, the resources of Ernst & Young offices worldwide and its more than 100,000 people deployed throughout 137 countries.

While Grand Cayman is small geographically (only a few miles wide and 22 miles long), it is a giant in international finance – by some measures the fifth-largest financial centre in the world. The Cayman Islands are the global leader in offshore hedge funds with an estimate of more than two-thirds of all new offshore funds worldwide being formed in Grand Cayman. Ernst & Young, Cayman is a leader in providing audit services to these funds.

In addition, Grand Cayman is home to hundreds of banks and trust companies, captive insurance companies, and a vigorous company registry as well as growing shipping and airplane registries.

What makes the financial sector in the Cayman Islands even more remarkable is that nearly all of its meteoric growth has taken place in little more than a generation. In 1965, for example, there were fewer than a half-dozen telephones on the entire island of Grand Cayman and only a couple of small banks.

A number of factors have contributed to this astonishing growth. For instance, there has been a mutually beneficial public/private partnership that informs progressive legislation, enabling the jurisdiction to adapt quickly to a changing global environment. Moreover, the regulatory regime, under the direction of the Cayman Islands Monetary Authority, is efficient and effective as opposed to onerous or punitive.

The Partners of Ernst & Young in the Cayman Islands. From left, Mike Mannisto, Rohan Small, Dan Scott (Managing Partner), Jeff Short, and Jude Scott

There has also been a strong historical bond with the United Kingdom. As an 'overseas territory' of Great Britain, the Cayman Islands enjoy remarkable stability that has evaded many other offshore jurisdictions. A highly respected local judiciary has ultimate appeal to Britain's Privy Council.

The Islands also have a peaceful population that enjoys racial harmony, very little crime, and one of the highest standards of living in the world. Last but not least, they have a well-developed professional infrastructure – equal to anywhere in the world – which includes sophisticated law and accountancy firms.

The early years

Ernst & Young, Cayman was both a pioneer and a trend-setter in the financial industry. The founding partners of the firm had a vision of building an organisation with roots going deep into Cayman soil.

One of the pillars of the practice is the shared belief that the firm has the obligation to identify and encourage the best and the brightest young Caymanian students to enter the accounting profession. The firm has been a leader in providing these students with summer jobs and later with complete university scholarships and virtually unlimited advancement opportunities. Almost all of the current leadership of the company have gone through this developmental programme. Partners believe that this recruitment

and 'incubation process' in large measure account for the success of the firm – and the individuals who make up its ranks. At Ernst & Young, Cayman, there is always collaboration, team building, checks and balances, and lively informed debate. What is never debatable, however, are the core principles of the firm: integrity, honesty, professional competence and a relentless quest for quality.

Operations Assistant Farah Joo with Office Manager Betty Ann Duty

Reading the signs

Ernst & Young is very aware that the financial regulatory landscape is continually shifting. It has therefore acted proactively to keep its clients in compliance with these emerging realities.

In the post-Enron/WorldCom era in the United States, the US Congress in 2002 passed the Sarbanes-Oxley Act, placing a much higher standard of independence on auditing and accounting firms. Importantly, in Grand Cayman, Ernst & Young has not only recognised this new imperative but has acted upon it.

In early 2005, Ernst & Young divested itself of its restructuring company which had been providing insolvency, liquidation, and forensic services to its clients. The firm, known in its early years as E & Y Restructuring (and later as Ernst & Young Ltd.), now operates under the banner of Kroll Cayman, an affiliate of Kroll Inc.

Looking forward, the partners of Ernst & Young, Cayman believe that clients will demand this degree of separation of their audit service providers from other such service lines.

Weathering the storm

On September 11, 2004, Hurricane Ivan, a Category 5 storm, pounded Grand Cayman Island for more than 13 hours with winds exceeding 155 miles an hour. More than 80% of the structures on the island were either damaged or destroyed – including the downtown offices of Ernst & Young.

Under the direction of Ernst & Young, Cayman's Business Risk Services team, which has been honing the firm's disaster-preparedness plan for years, the managers and staff provided uninterrupted service to their clients from temporary quarters set up in Bermuda. Within two short weeks, the entire staff had returned to Grand Cayman, and Ernst & Young was operating in full-service mode out of its downtown offices. There was virtually no downtime or compromise in the services provided by the firm.

Navigating the future

In the aftermath of the storm, the rebuilding process in Grand Cayman, structurally and economically, was both swift and effective. A new five-star resort, The Ritz-Carlton, Grand Cayman, is preparing to open its doors, the building of an exclusive Mandarin Oriental Hotel is moving forward on the eastern end of the island, and, perhaps most impressive, work has begun on the largest capital project in the history of the Cayman Islands.

The project, called Camana Bay, will be a totally 'new town' to be built in phases

Ernst & Young Partners 'break ground' for their new offices at Camana Bay in Grand Cayman. From left, Jude Scott, Rohan Small, Dan Scott, Jeff Short, and Mike Mannisto

A working session with (from left) Partner Rohan Small, David O'Donnell of the Audit Support Team, Partner Jeff Short, and Global Accounts Administrator Christine Rigby

over the next 20 years at a cost of approximately US$1 billion. Ernst & Young will become the 'anchor tenant' in the commercial centre of Camana Bay.

The partners and staff at Ernst & Young, Cayman have learned well the lessons of their seafaring forebears. They know that much in life is temporal. Storms may approach, seas may rise and risks – be they physical or financial – are sure to present themselves. We live, and have always lived, in a changing world.

What is unchanging, however, are the core principles that Ernst & Young, Cayman as a firm brings to these inevitable uncertainties. Like their sea-going ancestors, the firm's stewards always keep its ethical and moral compass set on 'due north'. It is the only way to navigate the economic, regulatory, and geopolitical waters in which we operate.

Cayman National Corporation's head office

Thirty years of financial services to the Cayman Islands

The Cayman National Group was founded more than three decades ago and is now one of the most dominant financial services providers in the Cayman Islands.

The organisation's initial strategy was to provide local and overseas clients with an alternative for their financial services needs, at a time when many international banks were being established in the Cayman Islands. Cayman National quickly established itself as a capable provider of financial solutions, giving quality service and innovative products.

The Group comprises six main trading divisions. Cayman National Bank (CNB), the best-known subsidiary, is one of the largest local retail banks, providing a comprehensive range of banking services though six branches. The only bank represented on all three of the Cayman Islands, CNB also has the most extensive network of ATMs there, with 14 ATM locations throughout Grand Cayman and Cayman Brac. CNB also offers full bank card issuing and merchant services, thanks to its in-house systems. It offers both Visa and MasterCard card services to its banking clients, and all major bank card brands to businesses through its merchant services support.

Full online banking services are also available through the bank's extensive online banking solutions, which can be accessed 24 hours a day, seven days a week through the Group's main website. The system is powered by leading technology and offers the highest levels of security and ease of use. In addition to the online services, customers also enjoy access to a sophisticated telephone banking system. Cayman National Trust complements the Group's banking products with full trust and

Mortgage finance for personal customers

Branch and offices at Edward Street, George Town

Banking hall in George Town

Corporate client signing for business finance

Leader in bank card services

company management services. Through this division the Group offers an extensive range of sophisticated products and services to both the local and overseas clients. This area of the organisation has recently seen considerable growth in its mutual fund sector, where the upgrading of systems and resources has prompted a large influx of business seeking high levels of services from a dedicated team.

The Group's securities and investment division, Cayman National Securities Ltd. (CNS), offers investment and brokerage services. CNS offers complete portfolio management services through its relationship with well-known and respected brokers worldwide. Clients thus benefit from the best international services available, whilst still receiving close attention from a small team of dedicated staff based in the Cayman Islands.

Whilst the Group's main activities are focused in the Cayman Islands, it also operates a full financial services company in the Isle of Man. The subsidiary Caymanx offers a full range of services in its own right, holding a licence as a financial services provider and a full banking licence.

The Group provides a full range of insurance products either through its brokerage company, Cayman National Insurance Brokers Ltd., or directly through its insurance company Cayman General Insurance Co. Ltd. (CGI). CGI is one of the largest locally based general insurance providers and offers health, property and casualty coverage to personal and commercial clients. It can also assist with insurance management through Cayman National Insurance Managers, which has more than 20 years' experience providing operational and financial management services for captive insurance companies with existing clients, including both local and international corporations.

In addition to the financial services products offered by Cayman National Corporation Ltd., the organisation offers an investment opportunity to local and overseas investors through its own stock. Cayman National is a publicly owned and traded company, with its shares listed on the Cayman Islands Stock Exchange. Shareholding is broad, with nearly 1,500 shareholders having an interest in the organisation. A covenant within its corporation constitution states that no one single entity or connected group can hold more than 10% of its shares. The company has a good record of profitability and dividend distribution and further investor information can be obtained from the Group's website.

Since its foundation, Cayman National has developed into a substantial operation, with the bank assets now approaching US$1 billion. This fact, coupled with its ability to offer a full and diverse range of financial products and services, positions the Group for many more years of continued success.

DISTRICT OF GEORGE TOWN

GEORGE TOWN

THE NATION'S COSMOPOLITAN CAPITAL

George Town is Grand Cayman's most populated district, with the nation's bustling and cosmopolitan capital at its heart. Long the seat of the Cayman Islands' Government, the district welcomes thousands of overseas visitors every year and accommodates a sophisticated and expanding business community.

Grand Cayman's infrastructure is centred in George Town and includes high-tech and reliable telecommunications and travel facilities. These are critical to the two main industries, international finance and tourism.

Over the last few decades, Cayman has evolved from being a relatively quiet group of Caribbean islands to the world's largest offshore banking centre, the second largest market for captive insurance companies and the preferred domicile for more than half of the world's hedge funds.

These companies are based in George Town and operate under the regulatory auspices of the Cayman Islands Monetary Authority. They are also serviced by a veritable army of professional and legal experts to keep the wheels of this thriving financial centre turning. As a result, the Islands have enjoyed spectacular economic growth and an unparalleled boom in commercial and residential development centred round the capital.

As the main port of entry into Grand Cayman, the town has played a major role in the expansion of Cayman's other economic pillar, tourism. Thousands arrive via the Owen Roberts International Airport or on the huge cruise ships that anchor out in the bay. Many are eager to make the most of Cayman's duty-free tax status. The majority of stores – selling everything from perfume to prestige Swiss watches and diamond jewellery – are to be found in plush shopping malls in town or situated along Seven Mile Beach. Both the town and Seven Mile Beach are home to the majority of the island's leading hotels, including The Ritz-Carlton, Grand Cayman Marriott Beach Resort and the Grand Caymanian Beach Club and Resort. There is also a wide selection of fine restaurants and bars in the district, catering to every taste and pocket.

Significant numbers of tourists visit Cayman for scuba diving. The pristine waters around George Town conceal a wealth of interesting sites for divers and snorkellers to explore – from coral reefs to grottoes, and subsea walls to old shipwrecks teeming with colourful marine life. In a quiet residential area south of the town, Sunset House is a resort reputed for being run by divers for divers, with its own accommodation and restaurant. World-famous Stingray City, a site just a short boat ride away across North Sound, enables swimmers and divers to become temporary close acquaintances with some surprisingly friendly stingrays. Beautiful white-sanded Seven Mile Beach starts in the

Bustling South Church Street

district of George Town and continues on to West Bay. A mecca for holidaymakers and watersports enthusiasts, this beach and all its first-class hotels, shopping malls, restaurants and bars remain the jewel in the crown of Cayman's tourist sector. Yet the district has plenty of other noteworthy attractions. Foremost among these are the National Gallery, featuring works by local and internationally reputed artists, and the National Museum with its focus on Cayman's cultural and natural history.

A leisurely walk around the streets should also take in sights such as the timber-ceilinged Elmslie Memorial Church built in the 1920s by the renowned shipwright Captain Rayal Bodden, and the nearby Seaman's Memorial inscribed with the names of some 150 islanders who perished at sea. This monument stands close to Fort George, which overlooks the sea. The fort was built around 1790 to defend the island from Spanish invaders based in Cuba. Ironically, it was not war but the efforts of an over-zealous property developer that almost led to its destruction in the 1970s.

The modern Legislative Assembly building on Fort Street is the home of the country's Government. Only minutes away, in the vicinity of Heroes Square, stand a number of other important national buildings. They include the Town Hall – opened on Armistice Day 1926 as a 'peace memorial', the Clock Tower commemorating the reign of King George V, the Court House and the Library. Heroes Square itself marks Cayman's 500th anniversary, celebrated in style by islanders in 2003. The square has several monuments connected with the country's unique past, including a statue of James Bodden, Cayman's first national hero, and the Wall of History mural.

The Conch House on North Sound Road was built in the 1930s. Its walls are embedded with thousands of conch shells, a reminder of the importance of this local delicacy to restaurants around Cayman. A popular destination for visitors is Tortuga Rum Company's bakery, where they can sample rums and various flavours of rum cake.

Heading eastwards along the A5 into the quieter part of the district, visitors encounter one of the island's more historic areas. Prospect is just a dot on the map today, but a discreet monument marks the original site of a large 18th-century fort, a twin to Fort George, designed to protect islanders from marauding pirates.

The southern part of the district also hosts one of the island's best beaches at Smith Cove, especially popular with swimmers, as well as the Dart Family Park. A new local attraction is the Skateboard and Surf Park at Red Bay.

Government administration building, known locally as the Glass House

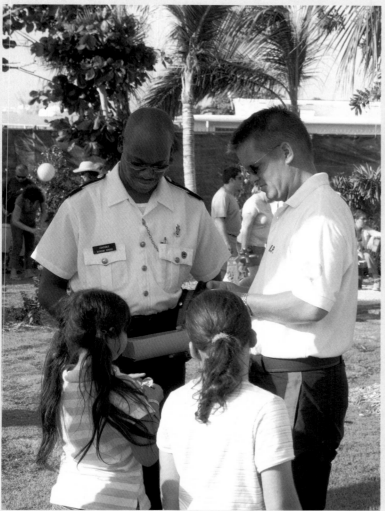
A safe environment

Elizabethan Square

GEORGE TOWN

Eco-tourism has become increasingly important in and around George Town as in other districts, and the National Trust works diligently to monitor and protect native flora and fauna. Close to Seven Mile Beach, the Butterfly Farm breeds and displays a variety of these beautiful and brightly coloured creatures. There is also a small wetland bird sanctuary at Spotts, not far from the district's border with Bodden Town.

Festivals have long been a key feature of Cayman life. Locals and visitors can let their hair down at the Batabano carnival, the island's major springtime festival. But the biggest public celebration is the Pirates Week festival held throughout the Islands every October. Its main event takes place in George Town harbour and involves an 'invasion' of authentic-looking swashbucklers. For those who miss this festival, there is always the possibility of a trip on the Jolly Roger pirate ship.

There is plenty to do for the sports-minded in the district. Golfers have the pick of two fine courses: the well-established Britannia and the new 120-acre course at The Ritz-Carlton, Grand Cayman,

designed by golfing legend Greg Norman. Because of Cayman's long association with Britain, there is even provision for the game of rugby, with playing facilities on the South Sound. As for runners, they get the chance to stretch their legs at the annual Butterfield Bank St. Patrick's Day 5K Irish Jog, which attracts residents and overseas participants.

Firmly ensconced in the 21st century, George Town is the hub of a dynamic economy that is globally recognised and admired. Yet to their credit, this unique Caribbean town and its district still retain much of their original island atmosphere, culture and joie de vivre – a fact appreciated by locals and visitors alike.

Duty-free shopping

A smile is never far away

0,0	110,0	Hn/FN/GM	Allg. Privatkundenbk.	119,19 G	119,19 G	119,19	119,19	119,19 G	±(	
5,0	431,0	F/KK	Allianz Leben vink.NA	505,00 bB	498,00 bB				-1,39	
5,1	480,0	S/FN	Allweiler StA	545,00 G	545,00 G			545,00 G	±(	
1,0	357,0	S/FN	Allweiler Vz	391,00 G	391,00 G			391,00 G	±(	
3,5	1,5	F/FN	Alno	1,60 B	1,60 -T	1,60	1,55	1,55 bG	-3,13	
6,0	21,5	H/FN	Alsen	22,00 G	22,00 G	22,05	22	22,05 bG	+0,23	
			Altenb.u.Strals.Sp. i.A.**	9,00 -T	9,00	9		9,00 -T		
9,3										
1,6										
1,0										
8,0	86,0	M/FN	AnterraVerm.**	103,33 G	103,33 G					
9,9	19,0	F/FN	Anzag	23,50 -T	23,50 B					
0,0	68,0	D/FN/GM	Apcoa Parking	97,00 -T	97,00 -T			97,00 -T		
2,0					17,77					
0,0					60					
0,0	65,0	F/FN	Arbed (L)	150,00 -T	144					
7,5	1	F/KK	Archer-Daniels (USA)							
4,0										
4,3	0,8	F/GM/Sx	Arndt	1,00 TG	1,00 TG			1,00 TG		
1,6	0,0	F/FN/GM	Artstor	0,04 G	0,04 G	0,04	0,04	0,05		
4,8	2,8	F/FN	Asahi Kasei Corp. (J)	3,60 -T	3,55 -T	3,55		3,55 -T		
20,0	250,0	F/KK	Asea Brown Boveri	270,11 bG	270,11 G					
20,0	13,2	F/FN/Sx	A.S.Creation Tapeten	19,10 G	19,10 bG	19,10	19,10	19,10 bG		
35,0	24,0	S/FN/GM	ATB Antriebstechnik	33,41 G	33,42 G					
28,5	17,3	F/KK	Atlas Copco A (S)	22,35 -T	21,60 -T					
27,2	16,2	F/KK	Atlas Copco B (S)	20,85 -T	20,25 -T					
95,0	139,0	D/FN/GM	Auda Classic Plc (i)	165,00 G	165,00 G	165		165,00 G		
5,0	67,1	F/KK	Audi	202,00 bG	201,00 bB					
6,0	1,5	M/KK	Augsb. Kammgarn**	1,50 B						
2,5	10,0	F/GM/Sx	Autania	10,20	0,30 G					
7,5	4,5	F/FN	A.A.A. Anlageverw.	5,15 G	5,15 G					
7,0	12,5	D/FN	Aach. Strb.	12,50 -T	12,50 -T					
58,0	370,0	D/FN	Aach. u. Mü. Leben	530,50 G	530,50	530,50				
74,0	250,0	F/KK	Aach. u. Mü. Vers.	353,50 -T	353,50 -T					
20,0	14,0	F/FN	Aareal Bank	16,20 G	16,00					
1,2	0,1	F/GM	Abacho	0,18	0,17 G					
6,4	6,4	F/FN	ABB Ltd. (CH)	8,90	8,80 -T	8,80				
22,8	15,2	F/FN	ABN Amro Hold. (NL)	17,50	17,10	17,10	16			
2,4	4,0	D/FN/GM	Actium Beteil.	4,80 -T	4,80 -T	4,80	4,80			
				7,00 -T	7,20 G					
			StA	6,10 B	6,30 B	6,30	6,10	6,10 bG		
				16,05 B	16,05 B	16,05	16,05	16,05 B		
			Estate	60 G	2,52 G					
				0,20 G	0,20 G	0,20	0,20	0,20 G		
			StA	20,00 TB	20,00 TB					
			)	19,00	19,00	19,40	18,40			
				29,85 -T	29,85 -T	29,85	29,85	29,85 -T	-0,1	
				18,00 -T	17,70	17,70	17,25	17,25		
			chnoSoft			3,60	3,60			

By Cindy H. Scotland, Managing Director,
Cayman Islands Monetary Authority

The Cayman Islands is recognised for its superior financial standards

Financial regulation
Working to the highest international standards

The genesis of the Cayman Islands' evolution into a world-class international financial centre began some 40 years ago, when a Banks & Trust Companies Law was established in 1966. Since then, the Cayman Islands has tailored its legislation to extend to a host of financial services including insurance, funds, trusts, company management, securities business, structured financing, vessel registration and stock exchange listings. Today the Cayman Islands is the largest offshore banking centre, the second largest market for captive insurance companies and is the preferred domicile for more than half of the world's hedge funds.

Modern and flexible

A modern and evolving regulatory environment has contributed to the successful development of the Cayman Islands into a leading centre for offshore finance. In addition, the provision of appropriate services and infrastructure, as well as operational flexibility, has helped the Cayman Islands achieve its elite standing in the global financial community.

As a British overseas territory, the Cayman Islands' legal system is based on English common law. The balance between sound regulation and flexibility is carefully crafted by the Government, the regulators and the private sector within a framework of clear and enforced legal and ethical principles in an effort to meet the demands of the international investors. Cayman's highly recognised regulatory regime is complemented by sensible legislation, rigorous law enforcement, and international cooperation involving bi- and multi-lateral agreements allowing for the provision of international legal assistance. As a result, clear and fair legislation with appropriate

cost-effective regulation and supervision can be efficiently developed to meet the changing needs of the global financial industry.

Factors attributed to the Cayman Islands' appeal for financial business include the pool of professional services offered, among them the services of lawyers, chartered accountants, corporate managers and other highly skilled service providers. Other key contributors to Cayman's attraction as an offshore financial centre include the existence of modern infrastructure, such as state-of-the-art telecommunications facilities and reliable utilities.

Ease of access is another major advantage, as there are direct flights to Cayman from major financial centres. Furthermore, the Cayman Islands share the same time zone with New York (EST), which is convenient for conducting business. The EST time zone is equivalent to GMT minus five hours, which facilitates business with Europe during morning hours. The sunny weather, world-class beaches and the safety of the islands add value to Cayman as an attractive jurisdiction in which to conduct business.

Sound supervision

Regulation and supervision of financial services in the Cayman Islands fall to the remit of the Cayman Islands Monetary Authority (CIMA), which directly oversees the banking, insurance, investments and securities and fiduciary sectors, in addition to issuing the Cayman Islands currency. The overall mission of the regulator is to enhance the economic wealth and reputation of the Cayman Islands by fostering a thriving and growing, competitive and internationally recognised financial services industry through appropriate responsive, cost-effective and efficient

supervision and stable currency. Since becoming operationally independent of the Cayman Islands Government in 2003, the CIMA has enhanced its ability to better meet appropriate international standards of accountability and transparency.

In performing its supervisory functions and to the extent that they are relevant and appropriate to the Cayman Islands, CIMA adheres to regulatory international standards. These include Basel Core Principles for Effective Banking Supervision, the International Organisation of Securities Commissions (IOSCO) principles for securities regulations, the International Association of Insurance Supervisors (IAIS) guidelines for insurance supervision and the 40 + 8 Recommendations of the Financial Action Task Force (FATF) dealing with anti-money laundering and combating the financing of terrorism.

In March 2004, the International Monetary Fund lauded the Cayman Islands' regulatory and compliance frameworks following its assessment of financial regulation and anti-money laundering in the jurisdiction. The IMF found that "an increasingly effective system of regulation, both formalising earlier practices and introducing enhanced procedures" was evident within the Cayman Islands regime. The report further praised the banking infrastructure, the high calibre of financial services practitioners and the jurisdiction's compliance culture in relation to anti-money laundering.

International cooperation

The Cayman Islands continues to advance its recognition in the global financial arena by constantly enhancing its cross-border cooperation and information-exchange agreements with other reputable regulators, while protecting legitimate privacy and due process rights. This commitment was formalised through the Monetary Authority Law, which requires the regulator to "recognise the international character of financial services and markets and the necessity of maintaining the competitive position of the jurisdiction from the point of view of both consumers and suppliers of financial services, while conforming to internationally applied standards insofar as they are relevant and appropriate to the Islands".

Presently, CIMA may share information with an overseas regulator in relation to matters necessary to enable the overseas regulator to exercise its regulatory functions, including the conduct of civil or administrative proceedings to enforce laws, regulations and rules administered by the overseas regulatory authority. This extends to client information, provided the overseas regulator has given proper undertakings with respect to confidentiality and use of the information. CIMA may also obtain information that is not in its possession by exercising its compulsory powers in support of an overseas request. CIMA's consent is required to any onward disclosure of information by the overseas regulator for the purpose of criminal investigations into breaches of laws or regulations administered by the requesting regulator. This ability to cooperate and share information with other supervisory bodies enables the Cayman Islands to continue its role in the global goal to ensure that financial systems maintain integrity and are used for legitimate purposes.

Anti-money laundering

Anti-money laundering is at the forefront of the regulatory culture in the Cayman Islands.

Through the prevention and detection of money-laundering, the Cayman Islands is able to preserve the integrity of the Cayman Islands' financial services industry whilst protecting the interests of stakeholders and maintaining the competitiveness of the Cayman Islands as a leading world financial centre.

Anti-money laundering legislation in the Cayman Islands has evolved over the years, beginning in 1985, when the Misuse of Drugs Law (MDL) was enacted to give effect to the Vienna Convention in the Cayman Islands. The MDL was concerned with drug trafficking and the laundering of the proceeds from such activity, and the law empowered the authorities to seize and confiscate drug trafficking money, and laundered property and assets. This was subsequently amended in 1992 to enable Cayman legislation to fully comply with the United Nations Convention against illicit traffic in Narcotics, Drugs and Psychotropic substances.

In 1986, the government signed a Mutual Legal Assistance Treaty with the United States that allowed for the exchange of information between the United States and the Cayman Islands in respect of criminal activity. This was then

CIMA issues the Cayman Islands currency

followed by a series of legislative measures aimed at stemming the flow of illegal proceeds into the Islands. On a broader level, the Misuse of Drugs (International Cooperation) Law (2000 Revision) provided for cooperation with other countries in relation to drug-related criminal proceedings and investigations. This cooperation is now extended to non-drug offences by the criminal justice (International Cooperation) Law (2004 Revision).

The Proceeds of Criminal Conduct Law (2004 Revision) (the 'PCCL'), one of the more recent anti-money laundering legislative tools, introduced "all crimes" anti-money laundering legislation and is the primary anti-money laundering legislation that covers all businesses and individuals. The money-laundering provisions in the PCCL apply to "criminal conduct" which is defined as an indictable offence if it had occurred in the Cayman Islands or conduct committed outside the jurisdiction that would constitute an offence if it had been committed within the Islands ("dual criminality"). The PCCL was subsequently revised in 1999, 2001 and 2004.

In 2000, a Code of Practice was issued to give practical guidance to financial services providers in the Cayman Islands in the prevention and detection of money laundering offences. The same year, the Money Laundering Regulations, 2000 ('MLR'), which was revised in 2003, was issued under the PCCL. The MLR places additional legal and administrative requirements on entities conducting relevant financial business, including due diligence. Of note, the Cayman Islands was the first jurisdiction to legislate retrospective due diligence on existing clients and to complete the exercise.

Conclusion

The Cayman Islands is committed to growing its thriving financial centre by building upon its political, regulatory and economic foundations. Financial institutions conducting business in the jurisdiction have come to realise that the success of the Cayman Islands translates to its success. It is one of the most mature and developed offshore financial centres in the world, and the formula for its continued success includes and will continue to be a proactive government, quality regulation, modern legislation, private sector excellence, flexibility, innovation and vision.

The Cayman Islands Monetary Authority building in George Town

Senior Partner, Nick Freeland (front); Paul Anderton, David Walwyn, David Walker (rear L – R)

Harnessing bright minds worldwide

After Hurricane Ivan devastated Grand Cayman in September 2004, triggering insurance claims of US$1.5 billion, professional services firm PricewaterhouseCoopers tapped into its worldwide resources to help banking and insurance clients deal with numerous challenges.

"Some clients lacked access to the sort of expertise available to us through our global network," says PwC Cayman senior partner Nick Freeland. "We called on that network to maintain the flow of their critical management information and the quality of their financial reporting."

A catastrophe is not, however, a prerequisite for getting assistance from PwC's global network. The firm's exceptional pool of international business know-how, experience, training and knowledge is permanently at the disposal of its clients. "If a client needs business-related advice about anything, anywhere, we make it our mission to get it," adds Mr Freeland. "With 122,000 staff in some 770 offices in cities worldwide, we usually find the answer we require. Our lead industry experts all know each other, so we know where to look and who to ask. By consulting our partners within our global network, we can give clients the benefit of different perspectives, fresh thinking and cutting-edge ideas. We use our collective expertise to give rock-solid

information and advice, on which vital business decisions can be based."

Information supply at PwC, known globally as Connected Thinking, is part of the firm's knowledge-sharing ethos. The firm responds to requests for business assistance, supplying clients and potential clients with a steady stream of pertinent information. It is the job of every partner, director and manager – from Paris to Panama, Beijing to Belgrade – to disseminate information to individual clients about new developments with a bearing on their businesses. That information goes beyond a client's particular industry, extending to geographical and demographic facts and emerging trends, be they local or global, which may be of relevance.

Sophisticated technology is used to integrate the Connected Thinking philosophy. Two major databases support the active sharing of information between all the firm's offices. They store details of numerous innovative business solutions and 'best practices', in fields ranging from accounting standards and banking to crisis management.

The same databases are frequently used by PwC staff in Cayman, where the firm's main practice is Assurance Services including statutory audits. Paul Anderton, a partner of over

13 years' standing, leads the assurance practice. The Cayman office's other practice areas are Corporate Finance and Recovery (CFR) and Company Administration Services (CAS), led by managing directors with international experience and outstanding qualifications.

David Walker, who leads the CFR team, has 14 years' experience in corporate restructuring and insolvency, gained while working in Australia, Canada, the United States, Indonesia and Thailand. He has advised many multinational and financial institutions, as well as the Australian government, on restructuring, credit and insolvency issues. PwC is uniquely positioned as the world's largest corporate restructuring firm to handle the most complex cross-border insolvencies, and the Cayman CFR team is a key component of that capability.

Head of CAS is David Walwyn, a compliance and regulatory advisory specialist. His former posts include a stint as deputy head of the United Kingdom government's Overseas Territories Department, where he oversaw financial regulation reviews.

Mr Freeland views his firm's future with confidence: "What differentiates us from our competitors is that while we have separate partnerships worldwide, as do many other multinational professional services firms, we have successfully developed and maintained very close links between our partnerships." He adds with pride: "Those links create a phenomenal resource which – underpinned by the proactive, multifaceted approach of Connected Thinking – plays a major role in maintaining our position as the global leader in our profession."

The legal specialists

Partner Hector Robinson with Senior Partner Charles Quin QC

Partners Neal Lomax, Kenneth Farrow and Q&H Corporate Services CEO Greg Link

One of the Cayman Islands' leading law firms, Quin & Hampson offers a full range of offshore legal services. Established in 1992, it has earned an international reputation for the quality of its legal advice. The firm delivers a professional, responsive and cost-effective service tailored to the needs of its clients, which include international and local banks, fund managers, investment advisers, international accountancy firms, multinational companies and high net-worth individuals from around the world.

The firm's lawyers, who work from modern offices in the heart of George Town, are highly qualified professionals recruited from top international law firms and barristers' chambers. The depth and breadth of their experience enables them to understand clients' businesses and to anticipate their needs. Languages spoken in the firm include English, French and German. It should be noted that Senior Partner Charles Quin, QC, is one of only six Queen's Counsel practising at the Cayman Islands Bar. The core practice areas cover banking, capital markets, corporate, insurance, investment funds, litigation, local practice, regulatory issues, structured finance and trusts. In addition, the firm's corporate services affiliate, Q & H Corporate Services, Ltd., offers a complete company incorporation and management service.

The Cayman Islands are the second largest offshore jurisdiction for all funds and the largest for hedge funds. Quin & Hampson has acquired extensive experience in the launch and development of local investment funds and its attorneys are able to assist in a wide variety of related areas, from the structuring of funds to their listing on the Cayman Islands Stock Exchange. The firm acts for leading sponsors, investment managers and fund administrators.

In terms of capital markets transactions, the Cayman Islands are the dominant offshore jurisdiction. In this field, the firm's attorneys provide advice relating to numerous forms of debt, equity and equity-linked transactions.

On the corporate side, the firm is experienced in establishing the various forms of corporate and other vehicles available locally, among them limited partnerships and unit trusts.

Being based in one of the world's leading financial centres, it goes without saying that Quin & Hampson also has significant experience in a wide range of finance transactions that involve the participation of Cayman Islands vehicles. Advice is available in relation to areas such as project finance, debt restructuring and the establishment and licensing of local banks. The firm acts for leading international investment and commercial banks, as well as substantial corporate borrowers and issuers.

The firm is also a leader in its other core practice areas – trusts, insurance, litigation and local practice. Its attorneys can, for example, provide advice on all aspects of Cayman Islands trust law. Moreover, they have extensive experience in civil, commercial and criminal litigation and the firm has been involved in numerous precedent-setting cases before the main local courts and the Privy Council in London, England.

Partner Angelyn Hernandez

Directors and staff of International Management Services Ltd

Offshore financial services pioneer

International Management Services Ltd ('IMS') is one of the largest company management firms in Cayman, providing services to more than 2,000 entities in the Cayman Islands and other jurisdictions, such as the British Virgin Islands and Turks and Caicos.

IMS has been in business for over three decades and formed over 5,000 companies for private individuals as well as multinational corporations.

IMS was incorporated in the Cayman Islands in 1974 by Paul Harris, a British chartered accountant who had originally come to the Cayman Islands in 1967 to open up the first fully staffed office of chartered accountants on the island, today known as Ernst and Young. He was also one of the first professionals on the island to concentrate solely on the actual management of companies on behalf of clients, rather than the provision

of third-party accounting, legal or banking services.

Today, operating from modern offices in a prime waterfront location in George Town, the firm provides a full range of company management services. These range from registered office only to full management, including provision of directors and accounting.

In 1976 IMS formed and managed one of the first medical malpractice insurance companies in the Cayman Islands, a highly successful captive that it still manages today. Since then it has specialised in providing management services to small boutique captives addressing the needs of select groups of physicians located throughout North America. The firm currently manages programmes writing professional liability business for doctors practising good

medicine in California, Washington State, Arizona, Illinois, Maryland, Virginia and SW Florida. All IMS client insurance programmes are underwritten by Lloyds of London syndicates. Michael J Howard has dealt with and been responsible for this section of IMS business since 1982.

In 1977, it registered Corporate Filing Services Ltd ('CFS') in the Cayman Islands. CFS provides statutory filing services, while IMS provides full management services, including directors.

Services were rapidly expanded over the next decade and, in 1988, the firm was one of the first to be licensed under the newly introduced Cayman Islands Insurance Law to carry on the business of insurance management.

IMS gradually began to provide fund services to hedge funds, and in 1994 it was licensed under the Cayman Islands Mutual Funds Law to provide operators (directors) for hedge funds. Although the firm now holds a full administrator licence, it restricts itself to the provision of independent directors who address the

Founder and Chairman Paul Harris

corporate governance aspects of funds administered by other licensed fund administrators. All members of the firm's funds department hold professional qualifications relevant to the services provided.

The firm has had a full-time compliance officer since March 2000. This important job involves ensuring that all matters of client due diligence, financial law compliance and anti-money laundering diligence are properly maintained as required by local laws and international standards. Certified accountant Cyrus Johnatty is the group financial controller and is responsible for maintaining the firm's complex financial record and information technology systems. Financial statements are filed with the Cayman Islands Monetary Authority and have been audited by KPMG for more than 20 years.

IMS has assembled a skilled and professional staff – with nine account managers and seven support employees – who well understand its many clients' needs. Clients, who are assigned to administration staff depending on the speciality required, range from investment companies to hedge funds, not to mention companies working in areas such as e-commerce, trusts, and ship and yacht registration. There is also a broad geographical spread of beneficial ownership and activities throughout the world.

IMS Directors Mike Howard, Insurance Division, Chris Bowring MD, and Ian Goodall, Shipping Department

The nation's leading company management firm

In order to be able to provide a complete offshore service to both its private and institutional clients, IMS has also obtained a full trust licence from the Cayman Islands Monetary Authority. This enables the firm to provide trustee services to complement the company management services that it offers.

Business is introduced by local and international lawyers, accountants, fund administrators, financial institutions and client word of mouth. The firm was also among the first significant offshore providers to offer its services on the Internet and today has an extensive website.

The firm is the Cayman Islands representative for most major international management companies from Hong Kong, Taiwan, UK, USA, Switzerland, Jersey, and Isle of Man among others. These activities are coordinated by Melanie Harris and companies can also be formed in other jurisdictions through the firm's close correspondent relationships.

Whether catering to professionals seeking to provide offshore services to their clients, multi-jurisdictional company incorporation providers seeking services in the Cayman Islands or advising individuals on financial services provided in the Islands, IMS is able to offer the same high-quality service that has established the firm in the forefront of offshore company service providers throughout the world of offshore finance.

Mutual Fund Directors: Phil Cater, Martin Byrne, Martin Lang

The company's Head Office

Heroes Square and Court House

Cayman Islands Public Library

The Town Hall, built as a peace memorial and opened on Armistice Day, 11 November 1926

HEROES SQUARE

Legislative Assembly Building

Government leader James Bodden, the country's first national hero

HEROES SQUARE

The Heroes Square Fountain

Wall of History mural, depicting 500 years of Caymanian history

Historic Milestones Wall and Court House

Clock Tower, built in 1937 to commemorate the reign of King George V

Cayman – bankers to the world

The world's largest offshore banking centre

Since its inception over four decades ago, the banking industry in the Cayman Islands has grown into one of the world's premier international banking centres. Also the world's largest offshore banking centre, the Islands are characterised by the presence of many of the planet's leading banks, a first-class professional infrastructure and a commitment to international regulatory standards.

The first real move to establish a financial industry in the Cayman Islands came in 1966 with the establishment of the Banks and Trust Companies Law. Today, in financial communities worldwide, the Cayman Islands are recognised as a foremost, sophisticated financial centre involved in a wide range of services.

Banking services in the Islands are provided via one of the two prestigious licences, either 'Class A' or 'Class B'. These licences are among the most sought-after banking vehicles internationally. Some of the benefits of operating a Cayman Islands offshore bank include the absence of capital gains tax or taxes on bank transfers and no exchange controls. There are also no property, capital gains or income taxes there. The country has enjoyed this tax-free status throughout its entire history.

There are currently in the region of 320 licensed banks in the Cayman Islands. Total bank deposits currently stand at over US$1 trillion and growing.

One of the key success factors behind the Islands' banking sector, and their financial services industry more generally, is the high quality of human resources. The country has a literacy rate of 98% and a flexible immigration policy that welcomes highly skilled professionals. Modern infrastructure and state-of-the-art telecommunications support the demands of international business, and residents enjoy political stability, social harmony and one of the region's highest standards of living.

The international currency

While maintaining their unprecedented success across a broad range of financial services, the Cayman Islands have maintained a centre of equally high integrity. The jurisdiction has spared no resources in securing a regulatory framework which is robust and has the respect of financial services professionals worldwide. Cayman was the first jurisdiction to voluntarily

open itself to inspection by the Caribbean Financial Action Task Force, the regional arm of the Financial Action Task Force. It has also been recognised by the FATF as a regional leader in the fight against money-laundering. The Cayman Islands also have in place a Mutual Legal Assistance Treaty (MLAT) with the United States and the United Kingdom, to set the rules and conditions for the international cooperation in the fight against crime. Recently a detailed IMF review of the Cayman Islands' regulatory framework for banking was carried out against the Basel Core Principles for Effective Banking Supervision, the international standard for banking regulation. In a solid endorsement of Cayman's high regulatory standards, the IMF report concluded that the Cayman Islands complied with every principle in the area of banking regulation.

Although privacy remains a cornerstone of a banker/customer relationship, as it does in other jurisdictions, the introduction of the Proceeds of Criminal Conduct Law in 1998 high-lighted Cayman's commitment to deal only with bona fide clients. To transact business in the Cayman Islands, a prospective client needs to be introduced to a banker who will ask for references which must clearly confirm a previously existing relationship with an onshore banking institution. The Cayman Islands Bankers' Association (CIBA), to which all major banks and trust companies belong, was founded in 1979. Its main objectives are to further the development of the Cayman Islands as an international banking and financial centre, to preserve the good reputation of the Islands, to liaise on behalf of its members with Government, business and other professional associations and to foster the education of people employed in the financial field. All members of the Association adhere to a 'Code of Conduct' which ensures adherence to high professional and ethical standards.

The Cayman Islands Bankers' Association is a member of the Cayman Islands Financial Services Association (CIFSA). This umbrella organisation was formed by a number of entities from the Cayman Islands' private sector, with the mission to communicate the integrity and quality of the financial services industry in the Islands to the global market place.

The jurisdiction has experienced consistently impressive growth within the financial services industry across all of the various areas of service over the past two decades. With its dedication to innovation and commitment to high regulatory standards, it is poised for further impressive growth rates in the foreseeable future.

Financial specialists offer sound and prudent advice for a global clientele

The Royal Bank of Canada was founded in the 1860s by a group of merchants in Halifax, Nova Scotia and is the largest financial services group in its home country. It is one of the world's leading banks, with some 1,300 branches and around 12 million personal, business and public-sector clients worldwide. Under the name of RBC Financial Group, it provides personal and commercial banking, wealth management, insurance, corporate and investment banking on a global basis.

The bank enjoys a close relationship with the Caribbean, having opened its first international offices there as far back as 1882. It celebrated its 40th anniversary on Grand Cayman in 2004. The company has tacked out in new directions since its inception in 1964. At that time, the Royal Bank of Canada was represented by a single bank branch in George Town. Today, three separate divisions of the company employ around 150 staff on the island, with a wide range of onshore and offshore financial expertise.

Royal Bank Financial Group's offices at Royal Bank House in George Town

An international banking pioneer

The bank's Cayman Islands head office and its main branch are in Shedden Road, George Town. It also operates another branch in the Seven Mile

Managing Director Ralph Awry (seated) with part of the management team of Royal Bank of Canada Trust Company (Cayman) Limited

Beach area, located at the Queens Court Plaza on West Bay Road, catering primarily to clients seeking personal banking services. Both branches offer a full range of local banking services, including credit cards, ATMs, personal loans and finance for house purchase.

The Shedden Road office is also home to RBC Dominion Securities (Global) Limited, Royal Bank of Canada's full-service brokerage, serving domestic and international investors, and Royal Bank of Canada Trust Company (Cayman) Limited which offers international high net-worth and corporate clients banking, trust, investment and fund administration services.

Private client services are always delivered through a Relationship Manager, tasked with tailoring them specifically to the individual's needs. The objective is to create, increase and preserve wealth, by offering services available within the Cayman Islands and

from other Royal Bank of Canada entities around the world. Review meetings with the client are held regularly to ensure that financial plans and arrangements match personal goals and economic conditions.

The company's strategic location and sophisticated infrastructure and experienced professionals allow it to provide world-class trust administration services. A key element of personal estate and tax planning, these structures are based on specific client need and the specialised trust legislation available in the jurisdiction. Additional services available for the private client include banking/credit, advisory and investment management.

A full brokerage service is offered to high net-worth individuals with international financial requirements. Expert Investment Advisors from Global Private Banking, the bank's international wealth management operation, actively involve clients in the decision-making process that leads to the provision of customised solutions.

A comprehensive range of services is also provided for corporate and institutional clients. RBC's local office has more than a decade of

Retail banking hall in Royal Bank House

experience providing fund administration services as well as comprehensive banking, investment management and credit facilities to corporate clients – all tailored to specific needs. Royal Bank of Canada is the largest provider of financial services to captive insurance companies in the Cayman Islands. The company provides

Investment advisor, RBC Dominion Securities (Global) Limited, Royal Bank House, George Town

captives with all the financial services they need to exist – credit, banking, investments and custody.

With a well-developed captive insurance infrastructure, a strong regulatory framework, and a favourable tax climate, Cayman is one of the world's best locations in which to establish a captive. Royal Bank of Canada works closely with these companies, giving them local industry expertise, combined with access to its global wealth management solutions and services.

Prudent management and the highest standards of practice are hallmarks of the Royal Bank of Canada worldwide. Over the last four decades, it has called on those strengths to build a highly successful business in the Cayman Islands and is today a vital part of the region's thriving offshore financial community.

A tradition of excellence

Incorporated in the Cayman Islands some 40 years ago, Butterfield Bank offers a comprehensive range of personal and professional services to individual and corporate clients. It is part of a dynamic group of companies that provide retail and specialist financial services in Bermuda, where it is headquartered, Barbados, the Bahamas, Guernsey and the United Kingdom.

The business originated from a merchant-trading firm that was founded in Bermuda in 1758. It became The Bank of N.T. Butterfield & Son a century later and was incorporated in 1904. Today the Group employs more than 1,500 people and administers assets in excess of US$90 billion.

Service – the key to success

Butterfield is one of the six clearing banks in the Cayman Islands. Reflecting its consistent growth and financial stability there, it has recently twice been named Bank of the Year. The award was given by the leading financial magazine The Banker, on the basis of the company's exceptional financial performance, its focus on innovation and customer satisfaction, as well as investment in the training and development of employees.

From its base in one of the world's leading offshore financial centres, the bank serves the retail, private, investment and corporate banking markets with a full range of services. These include mutual fund administration, retail banking, portfolio management, stock brokerage, treasury services, trust administration and corporate services.

Grand Cayman is home to five Butterfield offices employing some 300 experienced staff, with three retail branches. The bank's total assets in the Islands stand at US$2.3 billion, with client assets under administration at US$25 billion.

Butterfield Bank, Fort Street, George Town

On the investment services side, the bank provides discretionary portfolio management, brokerage and custody. It strives to build clients' wealth through diversified and flexible portfolios, achieved through consistent, above-benchmark returns at controlled risk levels.

The bank works closely with clients to meet their specific investment needs, through portfolio managers or a trusted network of services providers, brokers and international clearing houses. It also offers eligible investors a series of 14 award-winning mutual funds – among them money market, fixed income, equity, balanced and funds of funds – domiciled in Bermuda and Cayman and managed in-house.

The trust and corporate services are part of a range of the bank's private-wealth management solutions, for everyone from private individuals to international banks and corporations seeking a safe and secure home for their assets. Management teams can, for example, take care of all the business involved in setting up and managing trusts. In addition, they can handle everything to do with corporate administration – from the preparation of incorporation documents to the provision of company directors and a secretary. Further solutions include the administration of banks and trust companies, such as

Investing with a global perspective

Butterfield Online

helping businesses to establish an offshore presence easily and economically.

Butterfield Cayman specialises in providing administration of third-party offshore funds. Clients thus benefit from an offshore base, without the need for a physical presence. To that end, the company's experts deliver an extensive range of highly personalised and customised fund and corporate services.

The bank aims to provide quality service to a worldwide client base, through leading international correspondent banks, depositories and brokers. However, one of its key corporate values is helping the local community. This was recently underlined by its various generous actions designed to help the Islands' people and businesses find their feet after the 2004 Hurricane Ivan. Actions like these speak volumes about the unique attitude of Butterfield to business and wealth creation in the very widest sense.

The personal touch

Linburgh Martin, Managing Director, Close Brothers (Cayman) Limited

Close Brothers' office on the waterfront of George Town

The Cayman Islands arm of Close Brothers offers a comprehensive range of international financial services to a diverse and demanding clientele. Located in modern offices on George Town's waterfront, the company has enjoyed a presence in the world's premier offshore financial centre for more than three decades.

Close Brothers Group plc is the United Kingdom's largest independent banking group, with headquarters in London. It has total assets in excess of US$7 billion and features among the 200 largest companies, measured by market capitalisation, listed on the London Stock Exchange. Founded in 1878, it employs more than 2,200 people in its offices in the UK, Switzerland, Portugal, Germany, France, Italy, Guernsey, Jersey, the Isle of Man and the Cayman Islands.

In Cayman, Close Brothers provides bespoke asset management, fund administration, trust and company administration services. Together with its local banking affiliate, Close Bank (Cayman) Limited, the company focuses on institutional clients while also offering financial services to high net-worth individuals worldwide.

On the trust and corporate side, the firm prides itself on its personalised and dynamic service. Highly qualified advisors listen carefully to clients before deciding how to cater to their individual needs. Attention like this is especially important for trusts, since these flexible vehicles can be used for a broad range of goals – including wealth preservation, family protection and property holding.

The company provides a wide variety of trust services and can manage everything from private family trusts to life insurance and annuity trusts. Close also acts in a fiduciary capacity for structured finance vehicles, in securitisation and debt transactions, and also as an escrow agent and security trustee. For the many offshore companies based in the

Cayman Islands, Close has an extensive range of corporate services. They include company formation and a host of related management services, among them registered office facilities, company secretary and accounting. Cayman companies range from 'ordinary resident' and 'limited' through to the more complex, such as 'exempted' (the most common registration in the Islands), 'hybrids' and 'foreign companies'. Investment funds have flourished in the Islands as a result of the 1993 Mutual Funds Law.

The Close fund services team calls on sophisticated technology, as well as considerable experience in the alternative

Thiry Gordon, Deputy Head, Fund Services and Client Accounting

investment and offshore financial services industry, to offer an array of tailored services. They include administration for various kinds of structure – be it a mutual fund or trust, for example – to more specific services such as full accounting, net asset valuation and director provision.

Last but not least, Close Asset Management (Cayman) Limited provides investment advisory services to private individuals, trusts and institutions. To achieve consistent long-term portfolio performance for clients, the company can also call on its unique network of asset managers and investment products worldwide.

Great care is taken to provide customised programmes to meet each investor's evolving needs. This philosophy of personal responsive service underpins all of Close's operations in Cayman, so as to minimise risk and maximise returns for its growing client base.

A global presence

Serving clients in the Cayman Islands since the 1950s, Scotiabank offers a full range of retail, commercial and investment banking as well as international trust services through its trust division. The parent group is one of North America's premier financial institutions and Canada's most international bank, with assets of more than US$242 billion. It has some 200 branches in the Caribbean, 10 million customers in around 50 countries worldwide, and trades on the Toronto (BNS) and New York (BNS) stock exchanges

Scotiabank first opened for business in 1832 in Halifax, Canada before expanding into the United States and the Caribbean throughout the 19th century. In 1889, it opened a branch in Kingston, Jamaica, to facilitate the trading of sugar, rum and fish. It was the first branch of a Canadian bank to open outside the United States or United Kingdom, and formed the base of what would become a thriving network spanning some 25 countries throughout the Caribbean and Central America, making Scotiabank the largest bank in the region. In the 1960s and 1970s, the company extended its network into Asia and went on to expand its presence in Central and South America in

the 1990s, making it one of the world's most truly international banks.

Today, the Scotiabank Group's presence in Latin America is evident through majority-controlled Grupo Financiero Scotiabank Inverlat in Mexico, Scotiabank El Salvador, Scotiabank de Costa Rica and Scotiabank Sud Americano in Chile, as well as affiliates Banco Sudamericano in Peru and Banco del Caribe in Venezuela.

On the island of Grand Cayman, the institution's banking division employs some 75 people at three branches. In addition to its diverse range of personal and commercial banking services, the bank also offers comprehensive electronic cash-management services, including Internet banking.

Around 30 people are employed by the trust division, which operates at a single location. It provides private banking, management for companies, banks and trust companies, as well as administration for trusts, offshore mutual funds and pension services.

The bank has a long and proud history of supporting its local communities and is recognised as a leader among Canadian corporations for its charitable donations and

philanthropic activities, especially in the areas of healthcare, education and social services. In the Cayman Islands, it supports the local Crisis Centre Shelter for Battered Women, the Cancer Society, and Cayman Hospice Care. It is also an avid sponsor of sporting initiatives, among them rugby, basketball, volleyball and the Cayman Islands Little League baseball team, which is coached by employees of the bank.

Following the devastating Caribbean hurricane of 2004, the bank provided almost US$600,000 to relief efforts across the region, including a US$100,000 donation to the Cayman Islands Recovery Fund. Recognising the urgent needs created by the disaster, it responded both in financial support and by opening for business at the first possible opportunity.

Though an international bank with global reach, Scotiabank owes much of its success to the maintenance of personal contact with clients and it constantly works towards the goal of increasing their wealth. By skilfully combining traditional core strengths – including risk management, diversification and customer satisfaction – with innovative products and services, the bank is able to provide relevant solutions to clients' unique needs.

World-class network with local expertise

Established in 1996, Bank Austria Cayman Islands Ltd. aims to provide unsurpassed services to its portfolio of corporate and high net-worth clientele by offering a wide spectrum of banking services and investment products from its offices in Grand Cayman, in the Cayman Islands, the world's fifth-largest financial centre.

The Bank, which has a Category 'A' Banking Licence in the Cayman Islands, offers a flexible, friendly and personalised service. Its highly qualified and experienced professionals have extensive experience in banking and finance. A wholly owned subsidiary of Bank Austria Creditanstalt AG, a member of the HVB Group of Companies, Bank Austria Cayman Islands offers its clients all the benefits and resources of a world-class network of contacts, while maintaining a small bank feel and level of customer service.

The HVB Group – one of Europe's top five largest banking groups and ranked 21st largest banking group in the world (by assets) in 2004 – has more than 57,000 employees, operating 2,036 branch offices in 44 countries worldwide. With a staff complement representing nationals from seven different countries, Bank Austria Cayman Islands reflects the cultural diversity of a global banking group.

The Bank maintains a strong base of institutional, commercial and high net-worth clients and over the years has developed a diversified portfolio of principal investments. Moreover, it works with other members of the Bank Austria Creditanstalt AG and HVB Groups on a great deal of international finance transactions.

In its continued efforts to better serve the diverse range of institutional and commercial clients operating in the Cayman Islands, while also taking advantage of its position in the Bank Austria Creditanstalt and HVB Groups, the Bank has established a suite of banking and investment products and services which target Captive Insurance companies in the Cayman Islands. Insurance Captives are licensed private insurance companies established in the Cayman Islands that are owned and controlled by the insured parties and regulated by the Cayman Islands Monetary Authority.

The Captive Insurance industry continues to grow both globally and locally, with more than 5,000 captives worldwide. The Cayman Islands is ranked second in the world in terms of the number of insurance captives registered and is the undisputed domicile of choice for healthcare captives. More than 700 captives are registered with more than US$22 billion of total assets and collecting almost US$6 billion in annual premiums. Bank Austria Cayman Islands' goal is to help the Islands be a leader for captive services by offering a competitive and complete banking and investment solution.

The suite of products that

Whitehall House, the Cayman Islands office of Bank Austria

Success based on innovation

the Bank offers Insurance Captives and other institutional clients is broad-ranging and enables clients to handle all of their banking and investment needs without the hassle of involving sometimes several different service providers. The package includes full service day-to-day banking with web-access;

Every success starts with a vision

online statements; a selection of money market, fixed income, equity and fund-of-fund investment funds; letter of credit facilities (issued directly or confirmed by top-rated US banks); standard asset-backed commercial lending; tailored term deposit cash management programmes and full securities custody services.

The Bank's latest product offering is a family of investment funds managed by Capital Invest (Bank Austria Creditanstalt's fund management subsidiary). These funds include a US Dollar Money Market Fund, an Intermediate-Term US Bond Fund, and a US Equities Fund. The Funds are listed on the Cayman Islands Stock Exchange and available to qualified investors.

By calling on the vast network of resources of the Bank Austria Creditanstalt and HVB Groups, Bank Austria Cayman Islands is able to provide clients with innovative financial solutions. The Bank has enjoyed tremendous support from its growing institutional and commercial customer base in the Cayman Islands. It looks forward to continue offering world-class banking services, investment products, and innovative ideas deserving of the world's fifth-largest financial centre.

THE NATIONAL MUSEUM

The Cayman Islands National Museum is home to a magnificent collection of local arts and artefacts. They include everything from tiny coins to a typical island boat, not to mention numerous natural history specimens and rare documents. Many of these articles were acquired by the Government in 1979 from Ira Thompson, a passionate local collector. The museum opened in 1990 in George Town's Old Courts Building, one of Cayman's few surviving 19th-century structures. Its Natural History Exhibit includes a three-dimensional map of the undersea mountains and canyons around the Cayman Islands as well as displays of local natural habitats. The Cultural History Exhibition explains the lifestyle and traditions of Caymanians down the centuries.

Bathymetric map

Children's gallery

Exhibits change on a regular basis

The talking seaman

Family day out

Cayman Islands National Museum

Plaiting thatch for making hats, and other products

Museum shop

Art for all tastes

THE NATIONAL GALLERY

Artists great and small have regularly featured at the National Gallery of the Cayman Islands since its establishment in 1996. Located in Harbour Place, George Town, this dynamic institution is funded through government grants and private donations. It is dedicated to the local visual arts, promoting and encouraging Caymanian art and artists at home and abroad. The gallery holds up to eight exhibitions a year, some of them by leading international artists, and organises numerous workshops, lectures and community events. It also has a small gift shop and a popular art lending library.

'For Mangroves', by Chris Mann

School visit to the Gallery

"Well, I like it!"

Contemporary art

Viewing gallery

Artist David Bridgeman

'On the Rocks', by Charles Long

Artist Randy Chollette

Art exhibition

'Domino Game', by John Broad

The world's leading domicile for hedge funds

By Gary Linford,
Head of Investments &
Securities Division, Cayman
Islands Monetary Authority

Hedging risk is an integral part of the financial markets. Commodity traders began using forward contracts for protection against unfavourable price changes more than 200 years ago. But the term 'hedge fund' dates back as recently as 1949, when almost all investment strategies took only long positions. A reporter for Fortune magazine, Alfred Winslow Jones, pointed out that investors could achieve higher returns if hedging were implemented into an investment strategy. This was the beginning of the Jones model of investing.

Jones launched an investment partnership incorporating two investment tools into his strategy – short selling and leverage. The purpose of these two strategies was to limit risk and enhance returns simultaneously. He used an incentive fee of 20% of profits and kept most of his own personal money in the fund. This ensured that his personal goals and those of his investors were in alignment – a key feature of most hedge funds today.

Between 1966 and 1968, nearly 140 new hedge funds were launched as a consequence of the new dynamics of investing and managing money. Large hedge fund losses due to the 1973-1974 bear market caused many investors to turn away from these funds. For the next ten years, few managers could attract the necessary capital to launch new partnerships. By 1984, there were only 68 funds in existence.

In the late 1980s, a small group of talented hedge fund managers restored credibility to this product and attracted many of the world's best money managers away from the traditional institutional and retail investment firms. By the early 1990s, the number of hedge funds had grown to 500 with assets of approximately US$50 billion.

It was at this point that the Cayman Islands, an extremely successful financial centre and the world's fifth-largest banking jurisdiction, recognised the longer term benefits of diversification. In July 1993, the jurisdiction passed the Mutual Funds Law regulating mutual funds and mutual fund administrators.

Since inception, the Mutual Funds Law has drawn heavily on the principle of 'caveat emptor' with responsibility for due diligence of service providers, promoters and operators of Cayman non-public funds sitting with the investor. With non-public funds, the Cayman Islands has intentionally applied a far lighter regulatory touch – relying first on the internal governance procedures of the regulated fund and on market discipline to enforce laws and rules and to uphold standards. This is in keeping with the precept that primary responsibility for the conduct of a regulated fund lies with the fund's operator, not the regulatory authority, the Cayman Islands Monetary Authority (CIMA). The Authority will only take direct enforcement action when it believes the fund's governance systems and market discipline have

not been sufficient to accomplish this purpose. There are currently more than 6,215 regulated funds, and fewer than 5% are retail in nature. The vast majority fall within the broad definition of a 'hedge fund'. Growth has been phenomenal, with the number of funds almost doubling in the Cayman Islands over the last four years. The jurisdiction now has five times as many authorised funds as its nearest rival, Bermuda.

Most of the regulated funds originate with an investment manager or fund promoter in New York, London or Hong Kong. Almost every major city in the world probably boasts the management of a Cayman hedge fund. But the three major money markets mentioned above historically account for the establishment of approximately 75% of the funds in existence today.

A fund is defined under the Mutual Funds Law as any company, trust or partnership – either incorporated or established in the Cayman Islands, or if outside the Cayman Islands, managed from the Cayman Islands – which issues equity interests redeemable at the option of the investor, the purpose or effect of which is the pooling of investors' funds with the aim of spreading investment risk and enabling investors to receive profits or gains from investments. Recognising that a significant source of Cayman's hedge fund business is the United States, the Exempted Limited Partnership

Law of the Cayman Islands was intentionally based on the Delaware equivalent. The limited partnership is therefore very popular with US promoters and their advisers for investment fund structures such as master/feeder, multi-class, umbrella, multiple allocator and hybrid debt/equity structures. The CIMA has created a robust but flexible regulatory regime, allowing the Cayman Islands to quickly respond to new opportunities. Cayman's position as the domicile of choice for more than half of the world's hedge funds is in no small part attributable to the innovative environment that the CIMA has created, particularly in the requirement for all regulated funds to appoint a local approved auditor, the extension of segregated portfolio legislation to the funds sector and, more recently, the introduction of the Retail Mutual Funds (Japan) Regulations.

To ensure the effective discharge of auditors' obligations under the Mutual Funds Law and to enable an efficient interface with the CIMA, a local auditor sign-off is required on all regulated funds. Only auditors with a physical presence in the Cayman Islands will be approved. There was concern hedge fund operators would resist this policy when it was first introduced in 2002. However, the requirement has added integrity to the oversight offered to investors in Cayman-regulated funds and the policy has not been an impediment to growth, as

diligence within Cayman of local and foreign funds that are administered in the Islands.

There is clearly a symbiotic relationship between the Cayman Islands finance sector and the global hedge fund industry. The jurisdiction has provided a regulatory regime and professional infrastructure that has allowed the global hedge fund industry to flourish. In return the Cayman Islands has benefited from employment opportunities and revenue since this diversification was introduced in 1993.

The Cayman Islands has ensured it is flexible, pragmatic and maintains the right regulatory balance between the needs of fund promoters and fund investors. Yet it does so while embracing international standards that are applicable to each industry. The CIMA does not operate in a vacuum and has not ignored international standards set by the likes of the International Organisation of Securities Commissions and the International Monetary Fund.

However, the CIMA does not blindly introduce the standards laid down by the relevant international bodies. When considering such external recommendations, it recognises the need for proportionality and that any benefits to be obtained from amending legislation, regulation or policy should exceed the burden imposed on the industry. The CIMA is also aware that should the Cayman Islands wish to be a major participant in global financial markets, it cannot afford to ignore them. Cayman must engage with the relevant bodies driving the initiatives, improve their knowledge and understanding of the Cayman regime and help frame the discussions and craft the outcomes.

This philosophy resulted in the impressive 2005 IMF report that noted substantial observance by the Cayman Islands of the 30 IOSCO objectives and principles of securities regulations. In fact, only one of the thirty global standards was not observed and since the report the Cayman Islands has made a commitment to implement a number of recommendations made by the IMF. In many instances the Cayman Islands is ahead of the G7 countries. Take retroactive due diligence for example, where more influential onshore jurisdictions, such as the United Kingdom, opted not to carry out retrospective due diligence on their clients. The UK's main reasons for not doing so were the high costs and heavy burden to its financial sectors, which ultimately would be passed on to clients. Although this was the same cry from some of Cayman's service providers, in the end most absorbed the costs themselves.

The Cayman Islands has thrived as an international financial centre over the past four decades as a result of the Government, the regulators and the private sector carefully crafting the balance between sound regulation and competitive flexibility. There is no reason to believe this will change. With the likelihood of continued growth in the global hedge fund industry and with the Cayman Islands increasingly the safe choice for domicile, it appears as if this is one runaway freight train that will take a lot to derail.

evidenced by the 2,000-plus new funds since the policy became effective.

The Segregated Portfolio Company (SPC) was first introduced in the Cayman Islands in May 1998. The concept of an SPC is that a company, which remains a single legal entity, may create segregated portfolios such that the assets and liabilities of each portfolio are legally separate from the assets and liabilities of any other portfolios. The Companies Law initially restricted the use of SPCs to the insurance sector. But refinements to the Companies Law in 2003 have extended the use to investment funds, particularly in the context of multi-class funds that wish to prevent liabilities spilling over from one class to another. The relatively low cost of establishing new funds as separate portfolios and the statutory segregation between each portfolio have made the SPC structure the vehicle of choice for multi-class funds.

The Retail Mutual Funds (Japan) Regulations became law in November 2003. It aims to mirror the relevant Japanese securities laws to fast-track the required distributor approval in Japan for Cayman-domiciled funds. This legislative proposal was initially slow to be accepted in Japan, but there has recently been a flurry of applications by global top-tier financial institutions – again underlining the importance of the Cayman Islands embracing innovation and flexibility.

The 6,215-plus regulated funds generate significant employment and revenue for the Cayman Islands. Most funds, for example, pay registration fees to the Registrar of Companies and pay regulatory fees to the CIMA. They also employ a registered office provider, make use of a local law firm for transactions, compliance and notifications, and employ a local audit firm to sign-off on the accounts.

In addition, while not a requirement under the Mutual Funds Law, many funds employ one or more independent directors with a physical presence in Cayman and a locally based mutual fund administrator. They also make use of the cash-management facilities of a bank with a physical presence in the Cayman Islands to process subscriptions and redemptions, and they hold at least one board meeting in the Cayman Islands, making use of hotels, airlines and the local hospitality industry. The CIMA currently has over 145 licensed mutual fund administrators, including notable firms such as Admiral, BISYS, Butterfield Bank, Fortis, Goldman Sachs, RBC and UBS. The third-party administrator's role is important. It reassures investors that, in addition to the auditors, there is some form of independent oversight of the activity of the fund and its investment manager. Furthermore, the administrator reassures the CIMA that a regulated entity is responsible for client and AML due

Success built on

The office of UBS Fund Services (Cayman) Ltd., situated in George Town

A world force in banking, UBS, headquartered in Zurich and Basel, employs around 66,000 people, and has operations in 50 countries and in all major financial centres. The company is today one of the world's premier wealth management businesses, a global investment banking and securities firm, and a leading asset manager managing significant amounts in both single manager and fund of hedge fund strategies. It is renowned for its commitment to understanding clients' needs and a dedication to creating innovative, tailor-made solutions for them.

UBS Hedge Fund Services currently administers over 690 funds with assets in excess of US$94 billion, across some 20 markets. One of the top hedge fund administrators in the world, it has teams located in the Cayman Islands and Dublin, Ireland, headed by Managing Director Sean Flynn. Both the Cayman and Dublin offices, like those throughout UBS, call on state-of-the-art accounting and shareholder systems, so as to provide clients with a first-class quality service. The Advent Geneva fund accounting platform, for instance, is a real-time global portfolio system with features such as multi-dimensional reporting.

UBS Hedge Fund Services provides professional fund administration solutions to asset managers, investment banks and insurance companies around the world. As an integrated business of UBS, it is in a position to add value by drawing on the combined resources of all UBS businesses, including wealth management, asset management and investment banking.

Because the company has specialist expertise in both single manager and fund of hedge funds administration, it is able to provide facilities for both onshore and offshore funds. These facilities are backed up by the Group's first-class global infrastructure and support capabilities.

Located in spacious and modern premises in George Town's financial district, UBS Hedge Fund Services is ranked the number one fund administrator in the Cayman Islands. The Cayman operation offers a complete range of fund administration services to asset managers worldwide, including accounting, net asset value (NAV) calculations, registrar and transfer agency, and statutory and banking services. All of these have been tested over time, across multiple conditions and environments, to ensure complete client satisfaction. Around 120 highly qualified and professional staff focus on delivering exceptional client service, employing the latest accounting and shareholder technology.

In terms of fund and product set-up, for example, the company can work with a client's professional advisors to structure a fund that best meets the client's needs. Administration includes a wide range of accounting services, from NAV computation to calculation of fees and accruals including performance fee equalisation.

The company's shareholder services include maintenance of register of shareholders/partners and processing of all subscriptions, redemptions and transfers. On the statutory work side, the firm is able to provide a registered office, file regulatory returns to appropriate bodies, maintain all statutory records, bank on behalf of the fund and to maintain subscription/redemption accounts.

partnership

Last but not least, the company offers specialised services for funds of hedge funds. These include provision of credit lines for short-term liquidity management, foreign exchange facilities for currency hedging, and custody services such as trade execution and record-keeping.

Funds can be domiciled in the Cayman Islands and elsewhere. Besides providing superior administration services, the Cayman office holds a banking, trust and fund administration licence and is capable of fully servicing the banking and credit needs of every client's hedge fund.

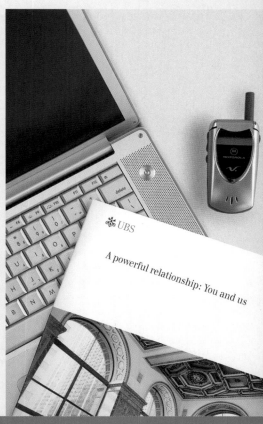

Why the Cayman Islands?

The Cayman Islands, notes Mr Flynn, are a natural choice for clients seeking a home for their hedge funds. More than 6,000 regulated investment funds managing assets mainly on behalf of institutional and high net-worth individuals are currently based in the Islands.

So why have they developed into one of the world's leading fund administration centres? The main reasons include the Islands' well-established financial services industry, enabling clients to benefit from a wide range of fund administration, banking, accounting, audit and legal expertise.

Investment funds domiciled in the Cayman Islands are not subject to statutory or regulatory constraints on their choice of investments, investment strategy, or the counterparties that can be appointed, such as investment managers, prime brokers and custodians. Fund managers therefore have a high degree of flexibility and control.

A number of other positive factors play in favour of the Islands. They are a politically stable British Overseas Territory. English is the official language of their business and legal community, with a court system based on the English model. All these factors, combined with the UBS commitment to listen carefully to clients and to work towards their success, make UBS Hedge Fund Services in the Cayman Islands the ideal port of call for those who seek the very best in hedge fund services.

The Fortis offices at Grand Pavilion in George Town

Over the last two decades, Fortis Cayman has become one of the leading financial institutions in the Cayman Islands. Ever devoted to customer satisfaction, it provides everything from administration and custody services to bridge and leverage credit facilities. It also intends forming in the very near future a dedicated trust company, catering for increased demand in the funds industry for trustee services.

The company is part of the Fortis Group, an integrated financial services provider active in the fields of banking and insurance. The group employs more than 52,000 people in over 200 companies worldwide and ranks among Europe's top 10 financial institutions. Its Cayman arm falls within the group's Merchant Banking division, which is part of the Alternative Investments Group. Originally incorporated in Cayman in 1984 as Pierson Heldring and Pierson (Cayman) Limited, the company became known in the 1990s as MeesPierson (Cayman) Limited. Following the international merger of MeesPierson with the Fortis Group, it was re-branded as Fortis Bank (Cayman) Limited in June 2000. At the same time, reflecting the growing importance of the fund administration business, a second company – Fortis Prime Fund Solutions (Cayman) Limited – was incorporated as a specialist fund administration and trustee business.

Fortis Cayman works through its parent group's Prime Fund Solutions global network, which provides services from key offshore locations (including Curaçao, Hong Kong, Ireland, the Isle of Man and Luxembourg) and has representative offices in Amsterdam, London, Milan, New York, Geneva, Frankfurt and Tokyo. This close relationship has allowed the company to specialise in the provision of an increasing range of services to the mutual fund industry. Most notably, the company has combined and consolidated a range of activities,

Serving the alternative investments industry

Network control room

The Accounting Department

Strategy meeting

The company is particularly proud of its efforts to promote Caymanian people within the organisation and offers a number of bursaries and scholarships. It also plays an active role in local society, having sponsored numerous sporting activities and purchased the boat for the Junior Sailing programme at the Cayman Islands Sailing Club.

Fortis Cayman's relationship managers have a deep knowledge of and commitment to issues facing the global investment industry. Working in a company where customer focus is a guiding principle, they therefore represent the perfect proactive business partner.

A well-motivated workforce

enabling it to provide an integrated package of services to hedge funds and funds of hedge funds. It is thus ideally placed to anticipate the changing needs of the fund management community as well as those of investment managers. Today the company is recognised as an industry leader for its solid experience and the service quality it offers to traditional and offshore investment funds. Fortis Cayman employs over 150 people in the Cayman Islands, with over 50 professionals made up mostly of accountants, lawyers and bankers. The growth in employee numbers has required numerous office moves, the latest being from central George Town to the prestigious Grand Pavilion Commercial Centre on West Bay Road. This relocation offered the firm an opportunity to expand and, because the building occupied was previously a hotel, employees enjoy access to some unique facilities including a pool, gym and café.

The George Town offices of BISYS at the Cayman Corporate Centre

Peter Young, Senior VP of BISYS Fund Services, Alternative Investment Fund Services and overseas BISYS operations in the Cayman Islands

Real leadership, real results

BISYS Alternative Investment Services is one of the industry's leading global providers of administration, accounting, advisory and tax services for alternative investment products. Investment managers of hedge and private equity funds, including fund-of-funds and other alternative investments, turn to the company for innovative and tailored solutions. Clients all over the world have entrusted it with the administration of more than US$200 billion in alternative investment assets.

BISYS Alternative Investment Services (Cayman), a thriving sector of BISYS, has grown to US$25 billion in assets under administration. The Cayman Islands is one of the fastest growing jurisdictions, which validates the company's strong position in the alternative investment marketplace. BISYS' (Cayman) global strategy is to continue to grow at an aggressive level.

The combination of dynamic management, a staff experienced in alternative investment and superior technology enables the company to exceed the standards of excellence its clients and their investors demand. In addition to providing general administration, the company offers technical services that encompass net asset value calculation, investor recordkeeping/reporting, tax recordkeeping, and corporate secretarial and director services. From maintaining the general ledger account and pending investor services to daily trade reconciliation and pricing, the company specialises in alternative investments and is expert in dealing with the various accounting and reporting requirements.

Additionally, the BISYS compliance program enables hedge fund managers to be prepared to comply with the ever-changing regulatory environment. The company has honed its legal, regulatory and compliance expertise through decades of experience, spanning multiple geographic domains. Offering a broad range of consulting and outsourcing services, it has the strength and depth of resources to respond swiftly and effectively to even the most complex compliance issues in multiple domiciles and jurisdictions.

The company's service model is distinguished by leadership and a deep knowledge of the alternative investment industry. Its team approach offers an uncommon degree of accountability. Seasoned experts collaborate to deliver advice and assistance on virtually any alternative investment issue – from setting up funds to day-to-day management of fund affairs.

For BISYS, it is all about building long-term relationships. Thanks to its expertise across the broad array of financial markets, it has the ability to reach deep into the many facets of a client firm and create strong, long-lasting relationships.

The company's contemporary reception area

Planning session

Admiral Administration Ltd was formed in 1996 to provide administration to a leading family of offshore mutual funds. The Cayman-based company has become one of the largest independent fund administrators, serving over 180 investments funds, with assets under administration in excess of US$20 billion.

The firm takes great pride in being completely independent and, unlike most administrators, is not affiliated with any large institution or prime broker. As a result, business comes almost exclusively through referrals from satisfied clients and other partners.

Over recent years, the offshore administration industry has grown significantly. Admiral attributes its success in this dynamic sector to an ability to focus on fund administration. "We keep it simple by providing only the services our clients want and need," says Canover Watson, General Manager.

Customisation is a key part of this proven business model. Depending on client requirements, the firm is able to deliver everything from basic shareholder-related services – which are especially ideal for start-up funds – through to full administration. The latter includes calculation of NAV (net asset value) and other more complex accounting services.

The head office of Admiral Administration in Grand Cayman

An independent outlook

All of Admiral's fund administrators are certified public accountants or chartered accountants. For the firm is of the opinion that the people in daily contact with fund managers, shareholders, selling agents and auditors should have a proven level of numeracy and strong communications skills. Mr Watson believes that this level of expertise and professionalism distinguishes the firm from any other mutual fund administrator, enabling it to identify potential problems and provide value-added services to clients.

Significant resources have been devoted to providing technical support and developing in-house software. Administration systems, for instance, integrate shareholder communications with financial record-keeping. The company's proprietary system tracks the flow of paperwork and funds from the inception of a transaction and produces appropriate correspondence to the shareholder (and selling agent) and updates financial records.

The system has other notable features. It can, for example, track the beneficial owners of investments, in order to provide fund managers with contact information not readily available from 'nominee-name' shareholders, with a view to client management and compliance with anti-money laundering legislation. Moreover, the system is able to monitor a variety of fees on a per-transaction basis, including sales commissions, client rebates and organisational changes.

Internet technology has been widely embraced for communication with clients. Consequently, the firm's rebilled charges are significantly lower than those of other administration companies. In addition, all incoming and outgoing correspondence is digitally archived.

The company remains committed to the Cayman Islands and recently purchased a 20,000 square foot building from which to conduct its expanding business.

Perhaps this commitment to the Islands explains why it is able to attract and retain so many highly qualified local personnel. This is unusual in the Caymanian financial services industry, notes Mr Watson, since most professional staff – particularly senior management and accountants – tend to be expatriates.

Whether clients are large or small, Admiral always puts their interests first. Its innovative services are customised to provide exactly what each client needs, instead of providing all services to all clients. For in the words of the General Manager, "We want to be the best at what we do."

Colourful beach and resort wear

WORLD-CLASS DUTY-FREE SHOPPING

Fine fragrances from La Parfumerie

Cuban cigar specialists, La Casa Del Habano

56

Rugs Oriental, the connoisseur's choice

Bernard Passman, for exclusive black coral

Artifacts, George Town's premier antique shop

Stylish duty-free gifts at Fossil Boutique

Clothes for the discerning at Arabus

Pure Art, the home of local arts and crafts

Gifts of distinction

Standing on the edge of George Town's harbour greeting residents and tourists with their iconic stingray fountain and palm tree-lined landscaping, Kirk Freeport's newest jewellery and specialty boutiques offer the Caribbean's largest collections of brand-name jewellery, watches, china, crystal and perfumes.

Owned by the Kirkconnell family, local business and community leaders for six generations, Kirk Freeport is recognised as a world-class marketplace by international designers and manufacturers of high-quality merchandise. The company has 22 stores, 18 of which are on Grand Cayman, and stocks the widest range of duty-free products in the Caribbean. The company is proud of its extensive collection of Rolex timepieces and is the brand's official retailer in the Cayman Islands. Besides offering famous designer jewellery, the Bayshore Mall store carries a collection of elegant watches, among them prestigious marques such as Cartier, Patek Philippe, Omega, Breitling, Tag Heuer, A. Lange & Sohne, Audemars Piquet, Vacheron Constantin, Breguet, Bulgari, Jaeger-LeCoultre, Panerai, Chopard, Piaget, Rado, Tissot, Baum & Mercier and IWC.

Showcases in the centre of the store feature some of the world's best jewellery brands.

These include David Yurman, Erica Courtney, Vera Wang, Roberto Coin, Waskoll, Stephan Hafner, Marco Bicego, Yvel, Pasquale Bruni, Rosi Blu, Oliva, Luca Carati, H Stern, Kabana,

Lagos, Favero, DiModolo, Damiani, Antonini, Aaron Basha. Adjacent to the jewellery and watch showcases is an impressive collection of crystal manufactured by Waterford,

Baccarat, Daum, Orrefors, Kosta Boda, as well as china by Versace, Royal Doulton, Herend and others.

Three other Kirk Freeport boutiques stand next to the jewellery store. The Lladro Boutique delights clients with one of the Caribbean's largest collections of Spanish porcelain figurines. The Lalique Boutique, as the name implies, will especially appeal to Lalique collectors and offers a breathtaking collection of jewellery, watches, crystal and home furnishings. La Parfumerie caters to men and women, with an open format that allows customers to sample any fragrance at their leisure.

Two blocks away on Cardinal Avenue lies a congregation of the company's boutiques and galleries, proudly bearing names such as Cartier, La Parfumerie I & II, Kirk Leather, Waterford & Wedgwood, Bon Voyage, Fossil, Swatch and Kirk Jewelers. Frequent visitors to the street sometimes refer to it as 'The Rodeo Drive of the Caribbean', because of all these prestigious offerings. Windows and marquees elegantly display products from companies such as Cartier, Rolex, Omega, Breitling, Tag Heuer, David Yurman, Roberto Coin, Mikimoto, Fendi, Longchamp, Guerlain, Liz Claiborne, Ralph Lauren and Tumi. Also on display are diamonds, rubies, emeralds, sapphires and other gemstones set exclusively for Kirk Freeport.

On entering the beautiful Cartier Boutique, visitors feel as if they have been magically transported to a luxurious Paris showroom. The Cayman shop is a temporary home to elegant jewellery such as Cartier's Trinity collection, Love collection and the Delices-Meli-Melo

collection. Another area features stunning watches including the Roadster, Tank Francaise, the Santos, and Divan. In addition, the shop offers Cartier leather goods and accessories such as pens, scarves, desk clocks and key-rings.

Visitors to any of the three La Parfumerie boutiques downtown have access to over 450 different fragrances for men, women

and children. Trained staff are on hand to offer guidance on the very best names in fragrances and cosmetics, such as Cartier, Calvin Klein, Lalique, Vera Wang, Yves St. Laurent, Tommy Hilfiger, Estee Lauder, Elizabeth Arden, Givenchy, Chanel, Ralph Lauren and

La Prairie. Frequently the perfume stores host professional make-up artists and celebrity appearances, to the delight of many regular clients.

The firm aims to cater for every taste and pocket. For clients not seeking jewels or watches, it offers Far East linen or locally designed T-shirts and clothing in the Far Away Places/Koko Tok store, located downtown on Shedden Road inside an old Caymanian home.

Fun souvenirs are provided by the Del Sol store down by the harbour. All the merchandise on offer here changes from black and white to blazing colour when exposed to sunlight. A major hit with tourists to Cayman, these goods include everything from T-shirts to shorts, tote bags, sunglasses and nail polish.

The best in brand-name luggage is available at the Bon Voyage store, while fashion jewellery, children's watches and Swarovski figurines are given prominence at the Jewel Trendz store. Last but not least, locally made souvenirs take pride of place in the Cayman Creations boutique.

Shopping for any of these goods is easy, with most of the stores located in central George Town. Other stores, all of which offer a mix of the firm's best-sellers, are located at the Owen Roberts International Airport departure lounge, inside the Westin hotel, at The Strand in the shopping mall, and on the island of Cayman Brac.

Having built the largest duty-free enterprise in the Cayman Islands from the humble beginnings of just a few jewellery counters in the community grocery store, Kirk Freeport founder Captain Eldon Kirkconnell is passing the business onto the next two generations of his family. Daily operations are now handled by Managing Director and Certified Gemologist Gerry Kirkconnell and by his sister, Director Debbie Guyton. Capt. Eldon's eldest grandchild, Christopher, has also recently started working in the company as the Vice President of Operations.

The family influence in the company is evident with every transaction. Thanks to their professionalism, expertise and devotion to clients, Kirk Freeport's sales staff are skilled at helping people pick the perfect gift whilst they enjoy one of the Caribbean's best shopping experiences.

Trusts in Cayman
Securing the future

By Patrick N. Bodden, Head of Fiduciary Services Supervision, Cayman Islands Monetary Authority

When you think of the word 'trust', you may think purely of the generic definition of confidence, reliance, hope, faith and dependence. However the word is also synonymous with one of the Cayman Islands' diverse offering of financial services products.

The trust, which was developed in English common law and allows for the separation of legal and beneficial ownership, has become a tool of choice for various applications within common law-based financial centres globally. As Cayman is one of the leading common law-based international financial centres, it is no wonder that a healthy trust services sector has developed.

Trust basics

Simply put, a trust is not a legal entity as is a company. Rather, a trust is created through an arrangement, usually formalised through a document known as the trust deed or the trust instrument. The arrangement imposes binding obligations upon a trustee to deal with specified property for the benefit of specified classes of persons or charitable purposes known as the beneficiaries. The person conveying the specified property to a trustee is known as the Settlor. The obligations imposed upon trustees and the powers conferred upon them are usually stated in a trust instrument and the applicable laws of the jurisdiction under whose laws the trust has been created. The Trust Instrument (Deed) is the governing document of the Trust to which the Trustee is obliged to adhere. The Settlor can provide a letter to the trustee upon creation of a trust, to highlight his wishes and his intentions for setting up the trust if he so desires. Trustees consider these wishes in their exercise of managerial and dispositive powers in the administration of the Trust. However, this letter, known as the letter of wishes, is not to be misconstrued as an instructional document to the trustee as it does not hold such powers.

Wealth management

Cayman trusts are created and governed pursuant to the Trusts Law that dates back to the 1960s. Cayman Trusts may be created to achieve a variety

Preserving family assets

Trusts, a key element in financial planning

of objectives in wealth management through a variety of inter vivos applications, where the property to be held in trust is conveyed to the trustee during the conveyor's (Settlor's) lifetime. In wealth management, trusts are also used for purposes of efficient succession planning, for preserving and managing the estate of the deceased, and a variety of other testamentary applications. With proper estate planning and long-term reliance on a product which can be passed through generations of a family for the protection and maintenance of those whom one wishes to benefit, then naturally the 'Trust' structure is a serious consideration and is normally a viable option.

STAR trusts

The Trusts Law was later bolstered by the introduction of the Special Trust (Alternative Regime) Law 1997 of the Cayman Islands (more commonly referred to as STAR). STAR allowed the Cayman Islands to offer a unique and more versatile trust product. This new regime allows for a number of variations to the traditional common law trust concept and affords local practitioners the basis by which to offer a variety of innovative trust products. This platform allows for the optimal use of Cayman trusts in the arrangement of financial transactions and the management of wealth for a cross-section of private and institutional clients. A major innovation brought about by the STAR legislation is the allowance for the creation of a trust for the benefit of a non-charitable purpose as well as persons. The characteristics of this regime allow it to be useful in satisfying the requirements of modern private wealth management structures. They also allow for the formation of trusts for certain commercial applications that satisfy specific institutional demands.

Cayman Trusts may also be used in a variety of commercial applications such as unit trusts as mutual fund vehicles and, increasingly, to facilitate transactions involving collateralised debt and asset securitisation. Cayman trusts are not required to be licensed or registered with any agency.

However, trusts may be registered as an exempted trust, allowing a trust to qualify for tax-exempt status. The provision of Trust services is a regulated activity.

Trust regulation

Since the introduction of the Banks and Trust Companies Law ('BTCL') in 1966, companies that provide trustee and other trust services are required to be licensed under that law and to be complicit with its provisos. The Cayman Islands Monetary Authority ('the Authority') is the autonomous regulatory body that has been charged with the responsibility for, inter alia, licensing and supervising trust companies in the Cayman Islands.

The Authority not only enforces the provisions of the BTCL, but also requires that licensees comply with other relevant financial services regulations and accepted standards of best practice. All companies that wish to engage in the provision of trust services, as it is defined under the BTCL, must become licensed and thus subject to regulation pursuant to the applicable laws. At the licensing stage the requisite due diligence and tests for fitness and propriety of the proposed principals is undertaken to determine the suitability of the applicant for licensing.

Many Cayman trust structures utilise the range of corporate vehicles that are made available through the Companies Law. These corporate vehicles are used to hold the assets of the trusts. Although the management of companies is an activity that is licensable under the Companies Management Law, a trust company that is licensed under the BTCL is authorised to provide company management services. The core business of the jurisdiction's licensed trust companies includes: the establishment of private trust and companies, the provision of trusteeship and directorship services, the administration and management of established structures, registered office and other corporate services.

In addition to good regulation and modern and innovative trust legislation, Cayman's appeal as a trust services jurisdiction of choice is enhanced by its excellent track record in providing top-quality trust services. Cayman boasts leading and internationally recognised trust companies and highly qualified and experienced professionals. Many of these are members of the internationally recognised Society of Trust and Estate Practitioners (STEP), which have a well-established branch here in the Cayman Islands.

Cayman's appeal and success as a trust jurisdiction is further enhanced by the jurisdiction's political stability and also our robust Anti-Money laundering (AML) and Combating Financing Terrorism (CFT) regime. These can only serve to encourage confidence in both the legitimacy of the jurisdiction and the integrity of its licensed services providers.

Through the decades, and with the development of a colourful array of financial products, the fundamental trust concept in the Cayman Islands still remains the same with the essential traditional components of lawful purpose, Settlor, assets, Trustee and beneficiaries, all being part of the Cayman Trust equation.

The CIBC offices in Grand Cayman

EXPERTISE IN OFFSHORE FINANCIAL SERVICES

Senior members of the financial team

CIBC Bank and Trust Company is a leading offshore financial service provider in the Cayman Islands. First established as a branch in 1967 in George Town, the bank is now a wholly-owned subsidiary of Canadian Imperial Bank of Commerce, whose roots stretch back to its founding in Toronto in 1867. CIBC ranks among North America's largest financial institutions with almost nine million personal banking and business customers.

With a highly qualified staff of over 100, CIBC Cayman is one of the largest financial institutions in the Cayman Islands. It provides a full range of banking, trust and investment services to individuals, corporations and international financial intermediaries.

In terms of company and trust administration, the bank offers its services to both individual and institutional clients around the globe, with special emphasis on clients from the United States, Canada, Hong Kong and the Middle East. Structures are set up to deal with a variety of issues arising out of cross-border immigration and investment, including estate planning and asset protection.

The bank also specialises in administration of special purpose vehicles (SPVs), for everything from debt restructuring to aircraft finance. SPVs are established for institutions seeking a stable jurisdiction with excellent infrastructure to set up

and administer complex commercial transactions and ongoing structures. Ease of planning is facilitated by the fact that the Cayman Islands have no income, corporate or capital gains tax.

Investment management is another area in which the company excels. Calling on long experience, it is able to customise portfolios to meet the specific investment preferences of high net-worth clients, including their individual risk parameters.

CIBC Cayman also provides extensive hedge fund and mutual fund administration services. It administers some 300 funds with total assets under administration of approximately US$8 billion. The fund department has about 40 employees, including 14 qualified accountants.

Funds under administration include a wide range of mainly institutional types, among them private equity, fixed income, and fund of funds. The full range of services available includes registered and records office alone through to full administration with audit-ready statements, banking and share registry and transfer service.

Because the bank combines fund administration with trustee capabilities, it can provide seamless administration services for funds which are structured as unit trusts and therefore require a licensed trustee. With the addition of its Class A banking licence, it can provide a true 'one-stop' service for fund managers.

The bank received 'Top Rated Status' in the recent 2005 Hedge Fund Administration Survey conducted by Global Custodian Magazine. As might be expected from an institution with roots in the Cayman Islands going back 40 years, it has historically been active in the community, participating in such programmes as Junior Achievement and Little League.

From its base in one of the world's foremost offshore financial centres, CIBC Cayman is determined to continue delivering banking, trust and investment services of the very highest calibre.

Investment Management department

Caledonian House, Grand Cayman

The Bank's senior management

International financial services

The Caledonian Group is a leading provider of international financial services that can trace its roots in the Cayman Islands to the early 1970s. Today this fast-expanding and privately owned Group offers a wide range of services through its various companies. Services available include banking, trust administration, investment management, fund administration, company administration and captive insurance management. Headquartered in the Cayman Islands, the Group also has offices in New York City and in the Isle of Man.

The Group is notable for its diverse client base which includes many of the world's top investment banks, hedge funds, investment advisors and high net-worth individuals. Besides being able to tap into the Group's wealth of expertise and global contacts, clients have access to Caledonian's wide range of integrated services, which are powered by the best-of-breed technology platforms such as Advent's Geneva portfolio accounting system and Infosys' Finacle Banking system.

Central to the Group's operations is Caledonian

Bank & Trust Limited which was licensed as a class 'A' bank and trust company in the Cayman Islands in 1988, entitling it to conduct all types of banking and trust business. Comprehensive banking and treasury services, some of them online, are offered to corporate, trust and institutional clients and to clients of Group companies.

Sophisticated and high net-worth investors utilise the investment department of Caledonian Bank & Trust Limited for dependable independent advice on international investment opportunities and for structuring and administering an investment portfolio.

Clients seeking trust and company administration rely on the company's diverse management team of professionals and a dedicated service-orientated approach to ensure the client's needs are met and that the administration of their company or trust is conducted to the highest standards.

Caledonian Bank & Trust Limited has over 15 years' experience working with many of the world's leading arrangers, investment banks and law firms in connection with the

management and administration of special purpose vehicles that are used in structured finance transactions.

Caledonian has been administering funds in the Cayman Islands for over a dozen years and provides services to a large number of investment funds through Caledonian Fund Services Limited. The services include fund accounting, registrar and transfer agency, corporate secretarial, web reporting and fund of funds custody.

Caledonian Insurance Services Limited is one of the largest independent insurance managers in the Cayman Islands. It employs a dedicated team of specialists with expertise in insurance management and accounting.

The Caledonian Group companies work closely with each other to provide a complete and unique offering of international financial services to Group clients. The management team is available to assist with the establishment of new structures and to advise clients how to take advantage of Caledonian's integrated offering, which results in a seamless and highly competitive service.

A global perspective

Partners James Bergstrom, James Bagnall, James Chapman and Peter Cockhill

The Ogier & Boxalls story is a textbook success case built from solid business principles and expertise. Established in 1991 as a niche firm, Boxalls (as it was then known) rapidly grew to become a major law firm in the Cayman Islands with a substantial client base, both local and international.

In February 2004, the firm merged with Channel Islands-based Ogier & Le Masurier, becoming part of the Ogier group, in a transaction which made international headlines as the first transatlantic merger of offshore law firms. This innovative step enabled the firm to enhance its Cayman capabilities by permitting clients to take advantage of a strong group presence in Jersey, Guernsey and London as well as, more

As with the global Ogier business model, the Cayman firm has two distinct arms: the legal services offered by Ogier & Boxalls and administration services by Ogier Fiduciary Services (Cayman) Limited. Both of these entities recognise that their businesses are 'people businesses'. They invest heavily in solid recruitment strategies, training and retention programmes to attract the very best people from major financial centres, so as to ensure that clients have access to the highest quality of offshore legal advice and fiduciary services.

Queensgate House, home of Ogier & Boxalls

On the legal side, corporate and financial law form the core of the practice, principally in the areas of banking, corporate, investment funds, real estate investment, regulatory advice and structured finance. At the same time Ogier & Boxalls is a full-service firm, with strong practices in the areas of immigration, litigation, private client, real estate and trust and estate planning.

Cayman's flexible but effective regulatory regime makes it the ideal jurisdiction for many investment funds, particularly hedge funds and private equity funds. Of the estimated 8,000 to 12,000 hedge funds worldwide, Cayman is

home to approximately 6,000 of them. With indications showing that these growth trends are likely to continue, Ogier & Boxalls is well positioned, with a significant market share as a result of its investment funds capabilities.

The banking and finance team advises blue chip corporations, international banks and financial institutions on securitisations and other structured finance products such as secured loan financings, establishment and maintenance of special purpose vehicles, capital markets, mergers and acquisitions and insurance. Ogier's presence in each of the premier offshore jurisdictions enables the firm to offer structured finance transactions that outperform other firms.

The administration branch, Ogier Fiduciary Services (Cayman) Limited, a sister company to the legal firm, has been providing management and registered office services to companies and partnerships since 1994 (originally as Ironshore Corporate Services). The company holds a mutual fund administrator's licence and a trust licence and is regulated by the Cayman Islands Monetary Authority.

With its strong ties to the Cayman Islands, Ogier remains an active community partner. It participates both financially and through the hands-on efforts of its dedicated staff in various community projects, including sporting, social and charitable organisations. There is a tangible commitment on behalf of the firm to contribute to the local community and to be active members of the Cayman society.

A welcoming smile

recently, New Zealand. The firm is therefore able to provide Cayman legal services from the American, European and Asian-Pacific time zones.

The move from a single-office practice to an internationally recognised global firm has expanded the reach of the services offered and has enhanced the firm's reputation for its commercial approach and the quality of its advice. Ogier – comprising Ogier & Boxalls, Ogier & Le Masurier and Ogier Fiduciary Services – is a market leader in the offshore world. This is evidenced by the awards granted the firm by its clients, peers and competitors, including Offshore Law Firm of The Year - Chambers Awards 2004, Private Client Team of the Year - Legal Business Awards 2004 and Offshore Advisor of The Year - High Nets Awards 2004.

Lawyers William Helfrecht and William McDonald II

The George Town waterfront

GEORGE TOWN

Snorkelling in Miss Eden Bay

The Jolly Roger

South Church Street

A safe haven for visitors

Fun aboard The Jolly Roger

The 'Pink Ladies'

Fort George

GEORGE TOWN

Enjoying the George Town sun

Welcome to George Town, me hearties!

The fish market on the shore at North Church Street

Past and present

Evening drink at Rackam's

'Tradition' by Simon Morris, a memorial to the Caymanians who have lost their lives at sea

The legal system

A key element in the nation's success

By Grant Stein, Senior Partner, Walkers

The Cayman Islands legal system is a key element in creating a sound business environment for international financial transactions and the local economy. Freedom from direct taxation and flexible, innovative legislation together with high professional standards and responsiveness contribute to the Islands' reputation as a place in which to do business.

History, Legislative Assembly and courts

Our law is primarily based upon English common law and principles of equity. In addition, laws passed by the Legislative Assembly and a substantive body of local and Commonwealth case law have provided the Islands with a modern legal framework. British legislation does not apply in the Islands, save where it has been specifically extended to the territory. Although it has the right to veto local legislation, the British Government generally does not intervene in the legislative process.

The court system includes a Summary Court, dealing with petty criminal matters and minor civil matters, a Grand Court for more serious criminal and civil matters presided over by the Chief Justice and three Puisne Judges, and a Court of Appeal consisting of a President and three other judges of Appeal. The Court of Appeal draws its members from other Caribbean jurisdictions, the UK and Canada. The English Privy Council is the ultimate court of appeal.

Freedom from direct taxation

There are no income, capital gains, or inheritance taxes in the Cayman Islands. The Government mainly obtains revenue from stamp duty, customs duty on certain imports, and licensing and registration fees (such as trade and business licences, banking and trusts licences, and incorporation and annual fees on companies). Additionally, there are no exchange controls.

Investment funds and international financing

Cayman's legal system has many attractions for the structuring of investment/mutual funds, financing transactions (for example, the sale and purchase of aircraft and ships), and synthetic securitisation of pools of bonds or loans (collectively, collateralised debt obligations). More than 6,000 open-ended funds are registered under the Mutual Funds Law and Cayman is now regarded as the leading jurisdiction in the world for hedge funds. Numerous closed-end funds, which are not regulated, have also been formed. Both types of fund can be organised as a company, a partnership or as a unit trust. Segregated portfolio companies (SPCs) allow ring-fencing of the assets and liabilities of each segregated portfolio from those of each other portfolio and from the general assets and liabilities of the company. They were originally designed for the insurance industry,

Queen's Counsel Graham Ritchie QC, Attorney General Sam Bulgin QC, Ramon Alberga OBE, QC, Andrew Jones QC, Nigel Clifford QC and Charles Quin QC, members of the Cayman Islands Inner Bar

but any exempted company may now register as an SPC – which are gaining acceptance as an investment fund vehicle. Recently specific legislation was introduced to accommodate Japanese investors.

In aircraft financing the transaction will involve the transfer of ownership of the asset to a special purpose vehicle (SPV), which will acquire it with a loan from the lender. The plane is then leased by the SPV to a third party such as an airline, via an operating lease. For the lender, the off balance sheet structure has several advantages, and the structure established in the Cayman Islands is entirely tax neutral.

Setting up a Cayman SPV is flexible, quick and relatively inexpensive. The SPV can be formed in as little as 24 hours. That is often considerably quicker than other offshore jurisdictions, where there can be a need for an "in principle" consent from the local regulator.

Flexibility of legislation

The Cayman Islands are essentially an English common law jurisdiction. So the central issues of corporate power, directors' fiduciary duties, corporate personality, limited liability and corporate benefit are in all substantive respects the same as the position under English common law.

At the same time, our commercial legislation benefits from being much less cumbersome in many of the areas that have caused considerable difficulty and uncertainty under the corresponding English statutes. For example, the Companies Law provides that shares are redeemable not only out of profit but also from the credit balance on the share premium account, enabling an equity instrument to have much of the economic substance of debt.

Contractual subordination is given statutory force. This means that a priority of payments settled by a Cayman Islands borrower would be enforceable by creditors, even if those creditors lacked the benefit of an associated security interest.

The SPV is usually structured as an orphan company with the shares held on trust for either a charitable purpose, or for the benefit of the transaction itself; an innovation of the Special Trusts (Alternative Regime) Law which introduced purpose trust legislation in 1997. By separating the beneficial interest in the shares from their legal title, the SPV accounts do not have to be consolidated in the accounts of either the share trustee or the originator.

A creditor-friendly jurisdiction of choice

Our insolvency law is generally recognised as being creditor-friendly. We do not have any system of corporate rehabilitation such as the English 'administration' procedure or U.S. Federal Chapter 11 proceedings where a debtor can effectively 'freeze' the rights of creditors. For example, secured creditors are not prevented from enforcing their security in the liquidation of an SPV, liquidators cannot disclaim onerous contracts, and fraudulent preference rules only apply when a disposition is made with a view to preferring one creditor over another – it is not enough that an asset or payment was made in circumstances which resulted in one creditor losing out.

Features of Exempted Company

An SPV is usually incorporated as an exempted company under the Cayman Islands Companies Law. As such, it has a number of special features.

No government authorisation or licences are

A sound legal system

required to incorporate. The name may be in a foreign language, and special provisions apply for the inclusion of the Chinese form of a company name on the Certificate of Incorporation. A minimum of one shareholder and one director (which may be a corporation or other legal person), neither of whom are required to be resident in the Cayman Islands.

Though required to maintain a register of directors and officers, and all but non-profits must notify the Registrar of its contents, these registers are not available for general inspection. Directors have wide discretion in how they organise their meetings and dispatch of business. They must maintain proper books of account sufficient to give a true and fair view of the state of the company's affairs and explain its transactions. Accounts are not required to be filed or audited, unless the company is licensed under one of the regulatory laws, for example, as a mutual fund.

A register of shareholders must be kept but is not available for inspection by the public. Shares do not have to be paid upon issue and may be of any par value, in one or more currencies, or of no par value. Fractional shares are permitted.

The company must have a registered office in the Cayman Islands. Meetings of the shareholders and directors can be held anywhere in the world. On an on-going basis, the annual reporting requirements are minimal.

In a compromise between the needs of financial institutions involved in securitisation and a commitment to anti-money laundering, bearer shares may still be issued provided that they are held by an authorised custodian.

Liability may be limited by shares, or by guarantee, or may be unlimited. Hybrid companies limited by guarantee but also having a share capital are also permitted.

Ordinary companies may carry on business within the Islands. Ordinary non-resident and exempted companies may not carry on business in or from the Islands, except in furtherance of business abroad. Foreign companies carrying on business in the Islands must be registered.

Partnerships and local business

Exempted Limited Partnerships (ELPs) are very popular in certain types of investment fund structures. They are formed by one or more limited partners, whose liability for partnership debts is limited to the value of capital undertaken to be contributed, and one or more general partners who are jointly and severally responsible for all debts and obligations of the partnership. An ELP is not a separate legal person under Cayman law and must therefore enter into contracts and act through a General Partner. At least one General Partner, whether a natural person or not, must be resident in the Cayman Islands.

Businesses operating within the Islands are regulated by the Trade and Business Licencing Law and a further licence is required under the Local Companies (Control) Law (LCCL) if a business is not at least sixty percent Caymanian-owned.

The Cayman Islands government has committed itself to creating a positive, permissive environment to encourage the growth of e-commerce. It has passed legislation to this end in the form of the Electronic Transactions Law, the Computer Misuse Law, and the Information & Communications Technology Law.

Real estate

Real property, developed and undeveloped, in general may be freely acquired by non-Caymanians. The only significant restrictions are in respect of carrying out development of undeveloped property, purchasing an ongoing business and ownership of multiple rental properties, all of which will constitute carrying on business in the Cayman Islands for purposes of the LCCL. Licences should be applied for prior to acquisition of the property.

The Registered Land Law provides a comprehensive registered land system. Registers in respect of all parcels of land, developed and undeveloped, including condominiums, are open to public inspection. No legal disposition of real property may be made unless in accordance with the statute, and the prescribed transfer of land form used. Stamp duty of transfers is currently 5%. Mortgages over real property are effected by way of legal charge in prescribed form registered on title. Charges attract stamp duty of 1% or 1.5%, depending on the sum secured. There are no annual fees.

Visitors, residency and employment

The Cayman Islands' second major industry is tourism. Special provisions in the Marriage Law allow visitors to marry during a vacation or even a cruise ship stop. The special licence can be processed within a very short time, and the marriage performed immediately after.

It is unlawful for non-Caymanians to reside without permission, or to engage in gainful occupation without holding a work permit. The Immigration Law was significantly revised in 2003. The new law seeks to better balance political and economic interests with human rights issues, and clarifies what constitutes the right to be Caymanian.

The opportunity to apply for the right to reside permanently is open to persons with at least eight years of legal ordinary residence, spouses of Caymanians, wealthy retirees and investors/entrepreneurs. Criteria which the Board must consider are set out in detail. Wealthy retirees and investors/entrepreneurs receive a certificate valid for 25 years, with or without the right to work, as the case may be. Successful applicants in the first two categories receive residency and employment rights certificates.

The Labour Law provides a broad framework for employer-employee relationships, including specific requirements as to vacation leave, sick leave, hours of work, health safety and welfare at work and termination of employment. The Labour Relations Board was established to promote the improvement of labour relations, and is made up of a chairman and eight members, four being representative of the interests of employees and four for the interests of employers. If the Director of Labour is unable to resolve a complaint through informal negotiations, the matter is referred to a Labour Tribunal.

The law courts on Heroes Square

Combining experience and innovation

Ingrid Pierce, Mark Lewis, Jonathan Tonge and Iain McMurdo of the Corporate Dept.

Walkers' head office in George Town

Founded in 1964, Walkers has become one of the Cayman Islands' largest and most innovative law firms. It has enjoyed exceptional growth in the past 10 years and now operates from offices in London, Hong Kong and the British Virgin Islands.

Its dedicated management and licensed trust company, Walkers SPV Limited, was established in 2001. This company provides a full range of management, trust, administration and offshore directors services from offices in the Cayman Islands and in Tokyo, Japan.

The firm is dedicated to exceeding client expectations with exceptional service. Its success is reflected by the calibre of its lawyers and the clients it attracts. The majority of its lawyers are from the top City of London and international law firms. Clients include major financial institutions, trust companies and other fiduciaries, investment banks and managers, leading law and accounting firms, as well as major corporations and partnerships.

An extensive team of lawyers and support staff focus principally on corporate and international finance law, with an emphasis on capital markets and structured finance, asset finance and investment funds. The firm is also internationally recognised as having the premier insolvency and restructuring group in the

The reception area at Walkers' Hong Kong office

Cayman Islands. It has an experienced commercial litigation, private client and trust department, as well as specialist banking, trust disputes, e-commerce, insurance and regulatory groups.

Walkers consistently ranks in the number one tier of Cayman Islands law firms, according to all leading international legal directories and periodicals. Moreover the firm consistently

Sara Collins, Angus Foster and Sandie Corbett of the Litigation Department

appears at, or near, the top of the offshore finance league tables and is a leader in funds for fixed income arbitrage, fund of funds, and global macro funds – confirming its role in the establishment of many of the world's leading institutional hedge and private equity funds.

The firm is equally committed to the local community in the Cayman Islands and has a unique philosophy towards investing in the development and education of children. It recently launched the 'Walkers' Children & the Arts Programme' to encourage the greater involvement of youth in the local arts community. This programme resulted in the creation of the vast majority of the arts programmes that the firm currently funds.

The entire firm gets involved in this programme and provides public relations and human resources support as well as financial assistance. In order to provide children in the Islands with the very best in comprehensive and educational arts programmes, Walkers works very closely with the Cayman Islands National Gallery, Cayman National Cultural Foundation (CNCF) and Florida Theatrical Association (FTA). The Children & the Arts Programme, the first of its kind locally, has been such a success that the firm is now exploring the feasibility of expanding it to its other offices.

Walkers is a founder member of the Cayman Islands chapter of Hedge Funds Care, an organisation dedicated to the provision of support for abused children by the investment funds industry. Cayman was the first jurisdiction outside of the United States to establish a chapter of this well-known and respected organisation.

In addition, Walkers is the only firm on the island that has a dedicated criminal and legal aid department set up to offer legal support to the community by offering pro bono services.

The firm has taken a fresh approach to providing legal solutions for over four decades. It recognises the importance of promoting the Cayman Islands overseas and contributes significantly to the local economy and community each year. A winning blend of innovation, expertise and community awareness has afforded Walkers the success it enjoys today as the leading law firm in the world's leading offshore jurisdiction.

The offices of Solomon Harris situated in First Caribbean House, George Town

The winning team

Providing offshore legal solutions

Solomon Harris is a full-service commercial law practice providing effective offshore legal solutions. One of the Cayman Islands' leading law firms, it has clients that include international financial institutions, public and private companies, high net-worth individuals, other law practices, and accountancy and advisory firms. The firm continues to build on its reputation for excellence and professionalism. The 2003-2004 edition of Chambers Global – The World's Leading Lawyers indicated that in their research, the firm had "received a string of recommendations for its 'top-notch' corporate and funds work" and that "clients praised the 'entrepreneurial and responsive' attitude of its senior lawyers." The firm is also recommended by UK publications such as Legal500.com, Global Counsel 3000 and IFLR 1000 – The Guide to the World's Leading International Business Law Firms.

Well established with a high international profile, the firm prides itself on having one of the fastest growing practices in finance, securitisation and investment funds, advising on a significant share of all funds registered in the Cayman Islands. It also has a hugely successful litigation and alternative dispute resolution practice.

In keeping with the Islands' status as a leading offshore financial centre, the firm has successfully expanded both the range and level of its specialised services. It caters primarily for an international institutional base including banks, insurance companies and fund groups. The corporate department played a key role in establishing the firm's international reputation, dealing with a wide range of international financing and investment transactions.

While recognising that professional expertise is fundamental, the firm also believes the key to good client relations is a proper understanding of the business at hand and the ability to guide and respond to client requirements.

The litigation department comprises an experienced team of barristers and solicitors, including a Queen's Counsel, all of whom have appeared before both Cayman Islands and UK or Australian courts. Its lawyers hold English law degrees and each has been admitted to the Cayman Bar. The department regularly handles major complex multi-jurisdictional cases.

Led by a senior lawyer, who gained a regional reputation as a timeshare financing expert, the Private Client, Property and Planning department specialises in advising high net-worth clients on everything from real estate, banking, business licensing and immigration to asset protection, wills, inheritance and trusts.

The firm also has a strong banking department, advising on domestic and international banking matters. Its clients include most of the local and international banks operating on the Island. The firm's thriving captive insurance practice has grown in parallel with Cayman's insurance industry, one of the world's largest offshore captive insurance centres. The trust department's team of practitioners is headed by the firm's senior partner. This team works closely with international law firms in other jurisdictions to ensure that all transnational issues concerning overseas grantors, beneficiaries and trustees are properly covered. Their task is not only to assist individuals and families who wish to establish and maintain Cayman Islands law trusts, but also to counsel institutions contemplating structured finance transactions which may require the establishment of purpose or charitable trusts for off-balance sheet transactions.

The firm's founder, Sophia Harris, is well known in local and international business and Government circles, having served as president of both the local Cayman Islands Rotary Club and the Cayman Islands Chamber of Commerce. She has twice spoken before the United Nations Assembly in New York on important constitutional issues facing the Islands.

Partner Paul Scrivener, who joined the firm shortly after its founding, was previously a partner in Eversheds, the UK's largest law firm. The leading law directory 'Legal 500' describes him as "highly regarded, being singled out as a 'commercial centre of gravity' and 'an excellent lawyer'...".

Sophia Harris and Paul Scrivener

GEORGE TOWN

Elizabethan Square, home of the Crusader International Group

Leader in insurance management

Getting the strategy right

Crusader International Management (Cayman), Ltd. is an industry leader with extensive experience in the formation and management of captive and alternative risk structures for public and privately owned business entities. The company's experience and creative resources provide a knowledgeable and steady guide for businesses seeking effective, tailored solutions for their risk management needs. Prime advantages of Crusader are the organisation's ability to focus on the particular requirements of its clients, and the flexibility to offer the most appropriate response for a particular situation. The firm offers a range of services, including captive insurance planning and management, life insurance and annuities, deductible reimbursement policies and other specialised forms of alternative risk transfer.

As a member of Crusader International Group, the company is able to draw upon considerable resources to provide a full complement of insurance, wealth management and risk transfer services. The benefits of working with Crusader are backed by a reputation for high ethical business standards. The company also has excellent working relationships with regulators such as The Cayman Islands Monetary Authority and The Registrar of Companies, as well as with leading corporate law practices, accounting, banking and investment

houses in Grand Cayman and many international institutions.

Located in George Town, Grand Cayman, B.W.I., the company was founded in 1993 by Ian Kilpatrick, who has more than three decades of experience in international insurance and finance. Mr Kilpatrick was the founding Chairman of the Insurance Managers Association of Cayman.

As the world's third largest captive insurance centre, the Cayman Islands were a natural choice for the company's headquarters, as well

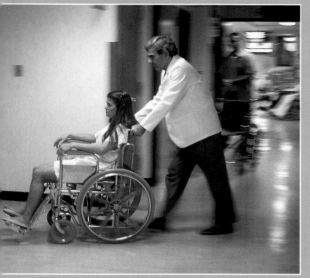

All aspects of long-term care coverage

as the headquarters of Crusader International Group. The Cayman Islands Monetary Authority, through its Insurance Division, regulates insurance companies under the Insurance Law of 1979. The legislation has been regularly revised, but is not unduly restrictive or onerous in terms of government regulations. An insurance

company formed in the Cayman Islands faces fewer restrictions than in many other countries, so it can insure or reinsure every conceivable type of risk. It can accept risks that the commercial market will not insure, including losses due to traditional risks as well as confiscation of assets, professional indemnity and product recall, to name but a few.

Captive insurance management is one of the services offered. The captive insurance market has expanded considerably over the last three decades, especially in the United States and the Caribbean, as a means for improved risk management. Captives offer better financial control, more responsive loss adjustment, as well as standardisation and simplification of loss and safety prevention programmes. In addition, a captive can tailor a policy to meet the specific needs of the insured, providing greater flexibility and reduced costs compared with conventional insurance markets.

For those interested in establishing a captive, the company offers comprehensive advice and assistance through its Design and Implementation programme. These services range from an analysis of the applicability of such a vehicle for financing of insurance risks through to incorporation of a new captive insurance company.

In addition to managing captives, Crusader is responsible for the administration of the many companies set up on behalf of its various individual clients. These include policyholders of the Advantage Life & Annuity Company SPC, a Member company operating an asset protection and estate planning service for worldwide clients. The company maintains a fully staffed office to ensure complete compliance with all

administrative and regulatory requirements. These asset protection, tax and estate planning tools for high net-worth individuals offer the insured the flexibility to customise investment options, while providing the tax advantages of traditional life insurance.

Chairman Ian Kilpatrick, MD Fiona Moseley and Director Michael Mead

Various reinsurance coverages

The company also offers deductible reimbursement policies and other specialised forms of alternative risk transfer. These policies cover a variety of property and casualty lines. Most risks are for coverage generally unavailable in the commercial market, but deemed important by the parties at risk. Clients can formally structure a programme to fit their individual requirements and loss histories by utilising the Group rent-a-captive mechanism, or can work with its knowledgeable staff to create unique solutions to their risk management issues. Samples of the typical risks covered include construction defects, a variety of long-term care coverages, business interruption and regulatory investigation.

The company's resources are enhanced as a member of the Crusader International Group, which has offices in Chicago, Scottsdale, Charleston and Washington, DC.

Committed to being the pre-eminent, privately owned insurance manager in the Cayman Islands, the company continues to enjoy significant growth and profitability. Clients are increasingly turning to it for innovative solutions to financial planning and asset protection, in the knowledge that these solutions are enhanced by the Group's strength and depth in international insurance, banking and investment.

Construction defects insurance specialists

The captive concept

By Seamus Tivnan, Insurance Managers Association of Cayman

A captive insurance company is a legal entity formed primarily to insure the risks of one corporate parent or a number of similar corporations (e.g. trade associations), thereby contributing to a reduction in its parent's 'total cost of risk'. Captives are usually domiciled in a specialised location, either 'offshore' (a country other than that of the shareholder(s)) or 'onshore' (a domestic jurisdiction).

Most, but not all, captives are established in an 'offshore' location. The main reason for this is not, as is often the perception, the desire to establish in a benevolent tax environment but because of regulatory issues and other business considerations. The recognised 'offshore' domiciles all have statutory regulation drafted with captives in mind and the regulatory authorities are used to dealing with captives. This reduces both the time taken to license a captive and the regulatory costs incurred by the captive in comparison with most 'onshore' locations. In addition, all of the established 'offshore' domiciles have developed an infrastructure of support organisations tailored to the needs of captives, thereby aiding a captive's ability to trade effectively and economically.

Captives are formed for many reasons. These include the lack of a commercial market for certain lines of coverage; the desire to recapture underwriting profits and investment income that would otherwise be earned by the commercial underwriter; a means to access the reinsurance market or, in certain circumstances, a means of diversifying into insurance services.

Captives are used extensively throughout the world by major corporations to cover risks situated both at home and abroad. The largest developments historically have been in the US, the UK and Europe, but recently considerable interest has been evident in the Far East as well as South America. As the trade barriers throughout the world are lowered and companies become more internationally oriented, insurance buyers are taking a more global approach to risk financing and captives can play an integral role in the successful implementation of a global risk financing strategy.

Cayman's Insurance Industry is regulated by the Insurance Law (2004), first introduced in 1979. Cayman's first captive insurance company was incorporated in the 1970s, prior to the introduction of the Insurance Law. That company is still going strong today. Since then over 1,000 captives have been formed in Cayman and currently over 700 captives are in operation in the jurisdiction, with more than 4,800 worldwide.

Cayman has always been a leading 'offshore' captive domicile, often seen as following in the footsteps of Bermuda – the country widely recognised as the domicile with the largest number of registered captives. Since 2002 Cayman and Bermuda have been 'neck and neck' in terms of new captive formations, with Cayman recently leading the world in terms of net growth. Cayman's popularity for this industry has grown year to year, for a variety of reasons. For example, it is a centre of excellence for service providers, has a stable economic environment, and a strong regulatory framework.

Traditional insurance

The commercial insurance market has high administrative costs which are passed on to their clients, the insured(s), within the premiums charged. Therefore, for every dollar in premium paid to an insurance company, that dollar is allocated to expected losses, administration costs and profit. In addition, the insurance company will take the premium and hold it until eventual payout – which could be many years. This holding of premiums gives rise to investment returns. The following demonstrates this.

Administration costs will include expenses such as reinsurance and commissions. Commissions are those amounts paid to intermediaries who find the business for the insurance companies (e.g. insurance brokers). Reinsurance is the amount paid

to other insurance companies who will accept some of the risk associated with the transaction or risk that the first insurance company assumed. These 'insurance companies' that support insurance companies are referred to as reinsurers or reinsurance companies.

Benefits of forming and owning a captive

The major benefits that the establishment of a captive brings to its parent can be divided into two main categories, financial and insurance. Financial advantages include reduced insurance costs, improved cash flow, matching of revenue and expense, and performance measurement. A captive can also be a source of additional revenue, for example expanding its book of business by offering insurance to related third parties.

There are many insurance advantages too. For example, a captive provides coverage for risks that are not usually insurable. Being answerable only to its parent, it can provide coverage that is not available in the commercial market or not available at a realistic premium. Other advantages include a reduced need for commercial insurance, an improved negotiating position, flexibility in programme design, broader and simpler insurance contracts and a better risk management programme.

How a typical captive operates

Generally, a captive is a fully owned, capitalised subsidiary of its parent company or association. It will be incorporated in a domicile appropriate to the captive's role in its parent's insurance programme and will be authorised to trade by the regulatory authorities in that domicile.

Control of the subsidiary will be exercised by a Board of Directors appointed by the captive's shareholders, generally the parent company. The board usually consists of a mixture of locally domiciled and parental appointees. It will, in turn, appoint selected local organisations to provide support services to the captive, including, if appropriate, attorneys, investment managers, auditors, bankers, etc. It is unusual for captives to appoint a management company to manage the company – as it is rare for captives to have any employees. The management company carries out all the operational functions on behalf of the captive and provides the insurance and other expertise that it requires. The scope of the management company's activities and the extent of its authority are defined by the board, to whom the management company reports, in the formal management agreement. Management reports are prepared by the captive's manager and it is usual for the manager to liaise with the appropriate parental departments.

The first name in group captive management

The George Town head office of the Kensington Management Group

Kensington Management Group has swiftly developed into one of the Cayman Islands' leading insurance management companies. Its diverse portfolio of captive insurers write in excess of US$600 million in annual premium, servicing the needs of more than 1,500 United States corporate clients. This represents more than a tenth of the total captive premiums written in the Islands.

Headquartered in George Town, Kensington is a full-service management firm, guided by the founder and President Michael Gibbs, a past Chairman of the Insurance Managers Association of Cayman. It provides a complete array of management and advisory services and coordination. These include captive feasibility studies, licence applications, captive formation, government/regulatory reporting and liaison, cash management, accounting, investment portfolio coordination, registered office and corporate secretarial functions.

At the firm's core is a senior management team with significant experience in the offshore finance and insurance industry. Each member also has a professional accounting qualification. Together with a further level of highly trained support personnel, these staff comprise the service teams for each captive client.

Through its association with Captive Resources, LLC, the acknowledged leader in providing consulting services to member-owned group captives in the US, the company has developed extensive expertise in managing group captives – an insurance or reinsurance company jointly owned by a number of typically unrelated companies, created to provide a vehicle to meet a common insurance need. "If structured the right way," says Mr Gibbs, "group captives can give small- and middle-market companies an opportunity to benefit from controlling their own insurance destiny, rather than being at the vagaries of the traditional market."

The captives market first burgeoned in the Cayman Islands in the 1970s. "The key advantages of doing business here," says Mr Gibbs, "include the strength and depth of the Islands' infrastructure, not just for captive management, but the one-stop shopping with the banks, mutual funds, stock exchange, investment houses, auditors and attorneys."

He adds: "The Cayman Islands' goal is to be recognised as the domicile of choice for all types of captive and for having the infrastructure and regulatory environment in place to facilitate this."

Kensington manages four of the world's top ten policyholder-owned captives. The largest of these, Raffles Insurance, has grown since 1985 from its nine original shareholders to more than 250 today, writing over US$170 million in premium annually. They operate with exposures and locations throughout the United States, in areas as diverse as manufacturing, distribution and contracting.

In addition to its expertise in group/association captive management, Kensington also has in-depth experience in single parent captive and segregated portfolio companies. They have a broad spectrum of coverages, including medical malpractice, workers compensation, general liability, product liability, auto liability and auto physical damage, property, employee benefits and warranty.

The company has long-standing relationships with other service providers, both in the Cayman Islands and overseas, including policy-issuing carriers, insurance brokers, risk control consultants, claims administration services, banking facilities, actuarial, audit, and legal firms. When establishing a captive, the company is able to ensure that the proposal is based on high-quality insurance business and that all the service providers used by the captive are considered as first class in their respective fields. Each service provider is expected to meet the aims and objectives established by the captive's Board of Directors and Kensington, through these relationships, assists the Board in ensuring the service providers meet those expectations.

Kensington meets and surpasses its clients' expectations for service quality by investing in modern technology, including customised software, as well as ongoing staff training and education. Far-sightedness like this enables the firm to control its own destiny and to successfully manage the insurance needs of all its clients.

Main Street

GEORGE TOWN

An aptly named coffee shop

The art of the cigar-maker

The Port Authority building on Harbour Drive

Street musicians

A budding artist

Island Glassblowing Studio

The junction of Main, Cardinal and Edward Streets

Smith Cove

GEORGE TOWN

Dart Family Park

Nasart Gallery

The Trolley Roger

Fashion show at the Paradise Grill

South Church Street

Traditional Cayman cottage

A cool glass of Chablis at Sunset House

CAYMAN'S ENTREPRENEURIAL SPIRIT

Someone once said that footprints on the sands of time could not be made by sitting down. Nowhere is this truer than in the Cayman Islands. As they advance from living in "the islands that time forgot" into the 21st century, successive generations of Caymanians continue to build upon the Islands' entrepreneurial traditions.

This entrepreneurial spirit dates back to an era when most Caymanian men went to sea for a living, leaving the women to raise children and protect the home front. Since those early days, ever-versatile Caymanians have seized every opportunity to improve their lives and their islands. Fishing, agriculture, thatch and jewellery-making soon became the norm and are still practised today.

Meanwhile, innovations associated with the Caymanian entrepreneur have flourished and expanded into many different ventures. Today, Cayman is a world-class tourism destination and a leading international financial centre. But the Islands' current success owes as much to the foresight of early industry pioneers as it does to continuing hard work and ongoing creativity.

And the results speak for themselves. The Cayman Islands enjoy one of the highest standards of

The Port of George Town

Cayman Islands' shipping registry, one of the world's largest for super yachts

Tortuga Rum Company, a leading exporter

living in the world and with an estimated GDP of US$2.0 billion in 2004, relatively low inflation, and unemployment under 4.5%, the fundamental strength of the economy is evident.

A British Overseas Territory, Cayman also benefits from a very stable political environment, one in which fiscal prudence is another well-established tradition within central government. In this setting, the US$3.4 billion damages inflicted by Hurricane Ivan in 2004 have been described by a leading international rating agency as "a temporary setback."

Apart from Cayman's excellent physical and professional infrastructure, one of the main factors attracting foreign companies there is the fact that the Islands remain a no-tax jurisdiction. The government does not impose income or corporation tax, nor capital gains, inheritance or gift taxes. There are no property taxes or rates and no controls on foreign ownership of property. The bulk of government revenue is earned through consumption-based taxes, such as licences, fees and custom duties.

Within this favourable environment, business ventures have flourished. Caymanian entrepreneurs range in age and ambition and are found in every sector of business, from recent high school graduates mesmerising tourists with their steel-pan skills to executives running multimillion-dollar enterprises. An estimated 51% of establishments are considered small businesses with ten or fewer employees; only 19% of all businesses in the Cayman Islands employ more than 25 employees. Possibly due to the seafaring tradition, which saw women remaining at home to "manage", female entrepreneurs are also predominant, outnumbering men by almost two to one.

Being silhouetted under the international spotlight, especially with regard to tourism and financial services, Caymanians have recognised the need to academically equip themselves to

State-of-the-art telecommunications technology links the Cayman Islands to the world

meet the needs of a vibrant economy. Two tertiary educational institutions – the International College of the Cayman Islands and the University College of the Cayman Islands – serve local needs and offer a broad range of academic courses. Caymanian students also study abroad and attend institutions regionally, in North America and the United Kingdom. The experience provides exposure to other cultures and practices, even as it equips them to contribute to the development of the Islands' economy. Local entrepreneurs

continue to reflect this emphasis on education, with roughly 47% having tertiary qualifications. The unique experience of living and working in the Cayman Islands attracts people from all over the world. Caymanians are culturally and racially mixed and embrace other nationalities, welcoming them to their islands. Some 60% of residents are locals, while the other 40% come mainly from North America or other Caribbean islands such as Jamaica. In all, more than 90 nationalities are represented in the total population, a diversity of

Owen Roberts International Airport, served by many international carriers

Local entrepreneurs are helped financially by the Cayman Islands Development Bank

St. Matthew's University School of Medicine

cultural influences that produce a fusion of music, fashion, cuisine and lifestyles. This melting pot is certainly a contributing factor to the creativity and innovation that continue to drive forward the Caymanian economy.

Recognising the increasing competitiveness of the 'global village', the Cayman Islands Government

has sought to become more proactive in enhancing and strengthening the local economy. To this end, the Cayman Islands Investment Bureau (CIIB) was established under the auspices of the Ministry of Commerce in 2003. With its mission of facilitating and securing appropriate long-term inward and local investment, the CIIB is an advocate for the continued development of the Cayman Islands' investment climate. Both local and foreign investors benefit from the CIIB

as a central point for resources and information relating to business opportunities in Cayman. Investors and entrepreneurs likewise benefit from the CIIB's active role in providing advice on policy and legislation that affect the operations of businesses in the Islands.

With so much to offer then, it is easy to see why the Cayman Islands achieve such a high level of success, and why the entrepreneurial spirit of its people continues to flourish.

A vibrant construction sector

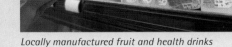

Locally manufactured fruit and health drinks

The dynamic city of George Town

ECONOMY

Tourism, the second pillar of the economy

A duty-free paradise

A world-class financial sector

GEORGE TOWN

GEORGE TOWN
BY NIGHT

By Valia Theodoraki,
Chief Executive Officer,
Cayman Islands Stock Exchange

The Cayman Islands Stock Exchange ('CSX' or 'Exchange') is an integral part of the Cayman Islands success story, catering for the specialist products of the jurisdiction. With its listings approaching 1,000, it has seen impressive year-on-year growth since it commenced operations in 1997. Thanks to its ability to successfully develop niche products and respond to changing market conditions, there is every reason to think that the Exchange will experience even more productive years in the future.

Mutual funds now comprise around three quarters of the total issues listed, making them the primary product of the Exchange. Mutual fund listings, the majority of which are institutional funds, include umbrella funds, funds of funds and master feeder structures.

We can attribute much of its growth to the alternative investments that have listed on the Exchange and in particular hedge funds, a product for which the CSX has gained a large market share in the world of capital markets. Major international banks and other multinational corporations have preferred the CSX as a listing venue for a variety of asset-backed securities, credit-linked notes and collateralised debt offerings as well as derivative warrants – all typically sophisticated financial instruments aimed at institutional investors. The granting of the 'recognised stock exchange' status by the UK Inland Revenue also contributed to a surge in demand for the Exchange's listing products.

The Exchange is a private limited company owned by the Cayman Islands Government but operating as an independent entity. The Stock Exchange Authority (the 'Authority') is responsible for its policy, regulation and supervision. The Authority reviews and must approve any rules which the CSX introduces.

The CSX is still a relatively young stock exchange. It was founded in July 1997 as a response to Cayman's dominant position in the mutual funds industry, to make Cayman more competitive on the world stage. Initially it provided a listing facility for the specialist products of the Cayman Islands: offshore mutual funds and specialist debt securities. Funds could this way be set up, domiciled, incorporated, administered and then listed all within the Cayman Islands, relying on the excellent professional infrastructure. Since then, the readiness to accommodate new products and structures has brought about new listing facilities for collateralised debt obligations ('CDOs'), derivative warrants, depository receipts, eurobonds and new rules allowing international equities to list.

The Exchange also offers special listing requirements to accommodate primary listings of preferred

The Stock Exchange located in Elizabethan Square, George Town

Stock Exchange
A continuing success story

shares issued by special purpose vehicles as well as debt and derivative warrant programmes. Another facility provided is a secondary listing facility for companies listed on another recognised exchange and an alternative-trading venue in the North American time zone for companies listed and traded on other recognised exchanges.

Experienced, client-focused, cost-effective

The CSX adheres to international standards. Its rules in the area of listing and trading are tailored to meet the needs of its customers, accommodating the latest sophisticated structures and products.

Listings on the Cayman Islands Stock Exchange are handled with professionalism, speed and efficiency. The Exchange's listing requirements are carefully balanced to ensure the safeguard of investors' interests and appropriate regulation, while at the same time encouraging funds through the flexibility of its rules to apply to list.

The Exchange combines several key elements

attractive to capital market issuers around the world, not least its ability to respond to changes in products and markets. Unlike European Union exchanges, the CSX is not bound by the EU Directives and is therefore much more flexible in its approach.

The listings meet the highest standards of governance and compliance, thereby ensuring that the Exchange maintains the faith of investors. The listing rules are also an ideal fit for predominantly institutional investors operating in sophisticated financial markets. As for the listing process, it is streamlined, ensuring all relevant information is disclosed without imposing unnecessary conditions and restricting issuers' activities. When it comes to listing of specialist debt securities, this may be effected by the issuer's lead manager or Cayman legal counsel to the issuer, dealing directly with the CSX.

The Exchange offers low listing fees and guarantees that the listing will meet each issuer's deadline.

The listing department staff understands the time pressures that govern the issues brought for listing and ensures that documents are processed quickly to accommodate the issuers' specific needs and timetable.

There are several other advantages to the CSX, such as the economies of scale in terms of no added cost of using another jurisdiction for listing when the issuer is domiciled in Cayman. Potential and current investors also get an added level of comfort that an issue is regulated and that an independent third party is monitoring compliance with the terms of operation stated in the offering memorandum. Lastly, a listing ensures a certain level of transparency and visibility, which is notably attractive to both future and current investors, and is an inexpensive and effective way to add credibility and a higher profile to a new or existing company.

The CSX staff is dedicated and professional. It has significant experience in capital markets and regulation, ensuring service from a team that understands the complexities of specialist products.

International recognition and membership

The Exchange is well regarded by international regulatory bodies. In 2004, the Board of the UK Inland Revenue granted the Cayman Islands Stock Exchange status as a 'recognised stock exchange' under Section 841 of the Income and Corporation Taxes Act 1988. The treatment of the CSX as a recognised stock exchange enhances its reputation and competitive advantage, placing the Exchange on the same footing as the Irish, London and Luxembourg stock exchanges.

In today's global marketplace, keeping pace with the latest innovation, regulation and trends is essential. Recognition of the CSX by the UK Inland Revenue confirms that it is an exchange of comparable merit and capacity to those in a major economy or significant financial centre. It also confirms Cayman as a global player with the regulatory and legislative framework necessary for the conduct of international finance and securities transactions.

One of the most significant memberships the Exchange obtained was in October 2003, when the International Organisation of Securities Commissions (IOSCO) voted to approve it as an affiliate member (the category available to exchanges). In addition, in June 2001, the CSX was the first offshore exchange to become a member of the Intermarket Surveillance Group. This is a group of self-regulatory organisations

The financial world never sleeps

committed to confidential market information sharing for regulatory purposes and to coordination of regulatory efforts among the various member entities.

Soon after it commenced operations, the CSX was admitted to the London Stock Exchange's list of registered organisations, making it the first offshore exchange to gain this designation. Securities listed on the Exchange are eligible for trading on the LSE's international equity market. The CSX is also a corresponding emerging market of the World Federation of Exchanges and a member of the European Securitisation Forum and the Asia Pacific Offshore Institute.

Recently the Cayman Islands and the Cayman Islands Stock Exchange were assessed by the International Monetary Fund in respect of the jurisdiction's regulatory and supervisory regimes. The IMF mission's assessment of the operations of the Exchange was positive, stating that the Exchange appeared to carry out its functions in a professional and competent manner. The assessors found that the listing rules of the Exchange provide for full, accurate and timely disclosure of financial results and other information that is material to investors' decisions. It also provides that all holders of securities in a company are treated in a fair and equitable manner. Accounting and auditing standards are in line with best international practices.

Technology

The CSX employs the latest and most advanced technology. It has developed a fully electronic web-based and order-driven trading platform. Trades are executed automatically when buyers and sellers are matched.

Great emphasis has been placed on ensuring that information concerning the activities of the CSX and its listed companies is accurate and promptly communicated to the market via its dedicated news wire service, which is also provided by Bloomberg. The Exchange has also recently developed a net asset value input system which enables fund administrators to input the information directly and ensure that net asset values are received, validated and communicated to the market without delay.

Our website mirrors information published on Bloomberg and provides interactive access to information and prices held by the Exchange. There are also links to research by leading offshore fund analysts, enabling investors to make relative comparisons between the performance of various funds and market sectors.

Although mutual funds have become the primary product, the Exchange, recognising the importance of diversification, launched in 2003 a crossing facility. This market is also web-based and the crossing rules incorporate enhanced transaction reporting requirements in order to adhere to the highest international standards. The CSX is uniquely positioned to accommodate trades that broker-dealers might seek to cross on a different market. For enhanced transparency, the cross-market activity that takes place is also submitted to Bloomberg immediately.

A bright future ahead

The Exchange is working towards strengthening its position as a first-class international exchange and it is anticipated that its market capitalisation will increase as the number of listings increases. It continues to look ahead and aims to preserve its exceptional growth so far. As the notion of a one-stop-shop is catching on with more and more issuers and investors recognising the benefits doing business in one jurisdiction, the economies of scale that Cayman offers will allow the Exchange to gain ground in both market share of listings and size.

The Cayman Islands Stock Exchange caters for the specialist products of the jurisdiction

The KPMG office in Grand Cayman

Thinking globally, acting locally

Partners of KPMG in the Cayman Islands

"Our advantage is that we combine local knowledge with international resources," says Theo Bullmore, Managing Partner of KPMG in the Cayman Islands. As a member of KPMG International, the global network of professional services firms, the company can draw on the expertise of nearly 94,000 people worldwide. "Our aim is to turn knowledge into value for the benefit of our clients, people and the capital markets," he adds.

The company has been established in the Cayman Islands for nearly 40 years and offers a full range of audit, tax and advisory services tailored to meet the needs of its offshore financial clients. "With a local staff of over 130 drawn from all corners of the world, regularly communicating and meeting with other KPMG member firms in the offshore jurisdictions, we can offer truly international advisory services

in many areas," says Roy McTaggart, Senior Partner. "Our areas of professionalism mirror the Islands' financial strengths – offshore banking, captive insurance and alternative investments."

A leading provider of audit services to the captive insurance market in Cayman, the firm calls on its dedicated insurance Partners Kevin Lloyd and John Ferrari to offer a wealth of industry-specific experience in this field. "The insurance industry is constantly evolving. We pride ourselves on aiming to deliver the independent insight and services our clients need, on time, on budget and with no surprises," says Mr Lloyd.

The alternative investments industry, primarily hedge funds and special purpose vehicles, has been a major driving force behind the continued development of the Cayman Islands as one of the leading offshore jurisdictions. The Alternative Investments Practice (AIP), under the leadership of Andy Stepaniuk, has spearheaded KPMG's efforts on a new global research report on hedge funds. It also participated in an offshore publication entitled State of the Alternative Investment Industry, Offshore which assesses this sector's trends and issues.

Doug Harrell, a Tennessee native, has been in charge of the firm's United States taxation operations for over a decade and is an experienced practitioner on US tax filing requirements for captive insurance companies, US individuals and hedge funds and their investors. The members of the firm's tax group

bring many areas of tax knowledge together to offer multifaceted insights into its clients' tax needs.

When offshore vehicles encounter difficulties, have simply run their course or would benefit from financial or operational restructuring, the firm's Corporate Recovery and Restructuring department, headed by Simon Whicker, is well positioned to offer assistance to investors, creditors or other stakeholders.

"Our aim is to maintain and enhance our reputation as the highest quality and most trusted advisor in the corporate recovery marketplace," says Mr Whicker. "Our broad range of skills and geographical experience reflects the needs of our clients." In addition to having core industry experience in insurance and other financial institutions, the firm's Corporate Recovery department has participated in the most recent precedent-setting cross-border cases involving Cayman proceedings in conjunction with US Chapter 11 proceedings, as well as s.304 insolvency proceedings.

In tandem with its multidisciplinary professionalism, the firm also feels a strong social commitment to the people of the Cayman Islands. This is evidenced by the time and resources it donates to education and training as well as the many hours that staff voluntarily contribute to community activities and projects. In recent years, the emphasis has been on sponsorship of sporting and developmental activities for the Islands' youth, to encourage both a sense of self-worth and the value of team-work.

Partners and staff having fun at a Caribbean theme party

Wealth management for private clients

Coutts (Cayman) Limited

Over 300 years of banking excellence

As one of the world's leading offshore financial centres, Grand Cayman enjoys an excellent reputation for the quality of its trustee and offshore banking services, with hedge fund administration playing an increasingly important role in the island's development. Although less well-known for wealth management, Grand Cayman still offers solutions for discerning private clients seeking access to top-drawer asset management expertise comparable to onshore financial centres such as Geneva, London or New York.

Coutts is a well-established international private bank which is part of The Royal Bank of Scotland Group, one of the world's largest financial institutions. It has had an office in the Cayman Islands since 1967, although its connections with the Caribbean go back much further than that. Indeed, they stretch back as far as the early 18th century, when one of the bank's clients, the Duke of Argyll, became a 'patentee' of the Jamaica Cochineal Company. Today, Coutts is at the forefront of international private banking, offering world-class asset management, banking and trust services. It provides tailored and integrated services to wealthy individuals who often have complex financial needs and, invariably, high expectations. These services are delivered via a network of dedicated private bankers supported by investment and trust specialists.

As a result of the trend towards greater sophistication on the part of wealthy private clients, the private banking industry generally has had to look closely at what clients expect. Quality of service is, of course, important. But investment performance is even more crucial in differentiating the strongest players.

Gone are the days when a private bank could rely on in-house resources to meet the demands of a sophisticated international clientele. In a world where specialism is the key to success, it is difficult to imagine any single provider being consistently excellent at managing different asset classes across global markets. That is why outsourcing is becoming more important as a way of providing access to world-class investment management expertise and research. When Coutts launched its own multi-manager programme in 1999, it was one of the pioneers of this approach. In 2005, for the third year running, Coutts won the prestigious Private Asset Management award for its 'Best use of long-only multi-manager' approach.

Coutts believes that the recipe for success is to offer, hand-in-hand with the highly personalised, tailored client service that has become its trademark, world-class investment expertise. Its dedicated private bankers have an in-depth understanding of their clients' needs, whilst outsourcing stock selection within various asset classes to those managers it believes to be leaders in their respective fields. Within individual asset classes and markets, the combination of different managers with contrasting but complementary strengths and styles can produce a blend which improves overall investment performance, while lowering risk. Alternative investments – as a separate asset class including private equity, real estate and hedge funds – add extra diversification to a portfolio (although some carry higher risk) and have the ability to generate gains even when markets are falling.

At Coutts, this diversification is then coupled with a robust and disciplined asset allocation policy to ensure that funds are efficiently allocated amongst individual asset classes and managers in such a way as to exploit opportunities – and reduce exposure to risk – as they arise in global financial markets. Together these are the key elements of a sophisticated and professional asset management service designed to produce superior investment performance over the long term.

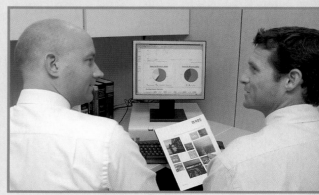

Private banking with a global perspective

Offices of Altajir Bank in Grand Cayman

PERSONALISED PRIVATE BANKING

Managing Director Rosaleen Corbin

From its modern offices in the heart of George Town, Altajir Bank has been serving small to medium-sized investors for some three decades. It provides clients worldwide with the personal attention and confidential services that only a private bank can offer.

The company received a Cayman Islands licence in 1974, to provide banking facilities to its corporate owners in Liechtenstein. In 1979, the owners increased the capital to US$20 million, creating a solid base for the accommodation of outside clients.

Altajir Bank is ideally placed to serve any person or company with funds arising offshore. Funds can be lodged with the bank in United States and Canadian dollars, Sterling pounds and Euro. The bank offers competitive interest rates in all these four currencies. Rates are quoted either on a term basis or on call.

There are no fees for opening or maintaining an account. Initial deposits of a minimum US$3,000 or equivalent are welcome, though sums below US$10,000 are kept on call. This policy underlines the company's saying that clients do not have to be 'high net-worth individuals' to bank offshore. There are no exchange control laws in effect in the Islands; therefore currencies can be switched to meet clients' requirements.

Term deposits are for three, six or twelve months. On maturity deposits are automatically rolled over for clients unless the bank is otherwise instructed. Call accounts are payable on demand, with interest computed on a daily basis, credited quarterly. Statements on call accounts are mailed to clients on a quarterly basis, unless some other arrangement is stipulated.

Deposit services are offered to any offshore individual who would like to build up savings for the future. It should be noted that the bank does not offer credit facilities or additional services, such as chequing, managed accounts, mutual fund investments, stocks, bonds or any other security trading. Debit/credit or ATM cards are not available.

Clients can deposit funds to their account by wire transfer or by international bankers' cheques. Due to recent legislation obliging Cayman Islands banks to have an understanding of their customers' business, Altajir requires a brief statement from depositors regarding the source of their funds.

Since customer privacy is protected by local law, for obvious security reasons the bank does not give out information on accounts or accept telephone instructions. All communication with Altajir is conducted through regular mail, courier services or facsimile. These tried and tested means enable clients to build a profitable and long-term relationship with one of the Cayman Islands' superior private banks.

The bank's reception area

GEORGE TOWN

Gateway to the Cayman Islands

George Town is the first port of call for the thousands of cruise ship passengers visiting Grand Cayman every day. Some two million arrive here every year, making this the world's fourth-busiest port for cruise ships.

The vast majority of these passengers, some 95%, disembark by taking a short ride to shore in a tender from their vessel. In the main they come from North America, travelling in style on ultra-modern ships that depart from Florida.

All of the major cruise lines call at Grand Cayman, including well-known names such as Carnival, Festival, Holland America and Royal Caribbean. Their cruise ships pay low tariffs – some of the lowest in the Caribbean – and no berthing charges, because they anchor offshore and are serviced by tenders.

Overseen by the Port Authority of the Cayman Islands, the port is busy around the clock. By sun-down all the cruise ships have moved on and it is the turn of the sea-freight vessels. These ships are loaded and unloaded at night by some 210 workers, who are split between the port itself and the Berkeley Bush inland cargo distribution centre. The port facilities can handle around

100 tons per hour. Due to the port's fairly shallow water, ships cannot exceed 6,000 tons fully laden.

In George Town, the loading and unloading of freight is handled by crawler cranes, able to make up to 27 moves per hour. This is a very high rate for such cranes, given that the larger and inherently faster gantry versions do not normally exceed 32 moves per hour.

The port takes pride in using only the very latest equipment and systems. Its forklifts in the warehouse are fully automated and drivers are obliged to use a code to log in and out. There are two sets of workers, waged and salaried, and the former clock in and out with a biometric fingerprint scanner – designed to prevent absenteeism and to discourage workers from leaving their posts early.

In line with the new, comprehensive security regime for international shipping, George Town port is fully compliant with the International Ship and Port Security Code (ISPS) for both ships and its own facilities. As a result, only ships that are ISPS-compliant are allowed to dock there. The local authorities also ensure security 24 hours a day, with closed-circuit TV at both locations. Moreover, all empty containers are checked for illegal cargoes before being redispatched.

A state-of-the-art computer system has been in operation since June 2002. This allows the Port Authority to handle a wide range of tasks, including security, accounting, the tracking of cargo and containers, and the keeping of up-to-date statistics. Customers of the port are also offered the convenience of tracking their own cargo through the Port Authority's website.

Number one in ocean transport

Thompson Line is the Cayman Islands' leading shipping company and one of the most important in the Caribbean. The family-owned business offers efficient and reliable transportation with its two state-of-the-art container ships – Shamrock and Caribe Legend. It is also active in the storage, handling and warehouse sectors.

The company's origins date back to the early 1960s, when Helen and Wilbur Thompson – who ran a successful grocery business in Grand Cayman – seized the opportunity to start a small shipping agency. The experience they garnered over the next 15 years dealing with cargo eventually encouraged them to lease a vessel of their own and to begin operations under the name Thompson Shipping in 1977.

The first cargo ship plied the route between Grand Cayman and Miami on a weekly basis. However, the burgeoning local economy soon led to demand for greater transport capacity and the family expanded its fleet with a number of other container vessels.

In 1980, Thompson launched its first regular shuttle service to the sister island of Cayman Brac. Over the next decade it added new routes to Florida and began operations to Costa Rica, bringing in cement for Grand Cayman's growing construction industry. In

1987, the company introduced its first versatile, multipurpose (including roll-on/roll-off) vessels. These were custom-designed in Germany to meet the diverse cargo requirements of ships docking at Caribbean and Central American ports.

In addition to focusing on its ships, the company added to its facilities ashore. Over the years, it has continually expanded its fleet of delivery trucks as well as its dedicated container and equipment repair facilities.

In 1996, the company entered into a joint venture with the Tropical Shipping Company, the largest containerised cargo carrier in the Caribbean region, headquartered in the Port of Palm Beach, Florida. As a result of this international link-up, Thompson today offers fast-ocean transit from Grand Cayman to Port Everglades and Tampa, Florida. To satisfy all the shipping needs of the Cayman Islands, the company is also able to call on the infrastructure of Tropical Shipping throughout the United States, Canada, Central and South America, the United Kingdom, Europe and the Far East.

To meet the local business community's needs, the company provides a range of comprehensive services. These include the ability to handle a wide variety of cargo with ease and care and transporting everything from small

packages and fresh produce to heavy machinery. In September 2004, following Hurricane Ivan, Thompson Line in conjunction with Tropical Shipping worked diligently to help with the recovery and rebuilding efforts in the Cayman Islands. It was also the first shipping company to make a landing on Grand Cayman, two days after the storm.

Thanks to its highly professional employees, Thompson Line has an extensive knowledge of shipping and local customs' regulations. This is all to the benefit of customers, who can expect shipments to be delivered on schedule from anywhere in the world. A fitting and ongoing legacy for a company whose homeland is justly proud of its 500 years of seafaring history.

Fuelling the Islands' growth

The Esso brand has been available in Cayman for over 70 years. Today the company operates 10 service stations in Grand Cayman, providing a range of high-quality products, first-class service and an enduring commitment to the local community.

The first drums of Esso gasoline were imported in 1930, but it was not until 1959 that the company entered the Cayman Islands and began construction of the Jackson Point Fuel Terminal on South Church Street. Since then, it has added to Cayman's infrastructure with the construction of service stations, continued incorporation of world-class technology and an underground fuel pipeline to the electrical generating company. It has also enhanced the Jackson Point anchorage to a modern and more eco-friendly seaberth for vessels up to 46,000 tons.

Esso introduced the first service station with Convenience Store in the mid-1980s to improve product offerings and meet increasing consumer demand. Significant long-term investment by the company in service stations provides Caymanians with exceptional business opportunities as service station dealers.

The latest Esso 'On The Run' C-Stores, for example, break new ground by offering food products in a 'fast, fresh and friendly' atmosphere. New state-of-the-art service station facilities also include double-walled underground fuel tanks with automatic leak detection and over-fill protection systems.

Hell Esso, Jack's, Mostyn's, 4 Winds, Delworth's, Brown's Industrial, Brown's Red Bay, 7-Mile Esso, Crewe Road Esso and Jose's have become destination points – not only for those wanting to refuel or grab a quick bite, but meeting places to relax and catch up with local gossip. Yet these stations' dealers do far more than just sell fuel or offer a friendly greeting and have helped the community in many ways over the years.

Back in the 1970s, service station owner Delworth McLaughlin owned the island's first radio telephone and relayed distress calls from sea vessels in trouble to the authorities, reportedly saving many lives. As for the owners of Hell Esso in West Bay – the Parson's family, Idalet and her three sons Astor, Aston and Arden, they annually organise Christmas parties for some 300 local children.

Primarily focused on education and helping children in school, Esso is also an active participant in 'Junior Achievement'. In collaboration with the local dealers, recent 'Help Us Help' promotional campaigns have helped the National Council of Voluntary Organisations and the Department of Education to meet the needs of schoolchildren requiring assistance with school supplies and provided Cayman's schools with computers and musical instruments. In a similar vein, the company supports Rotary's 'Meals on Wheels' programme.

The company is also active in sponsoring sports such as soccer, baseball, softball, cricket and basketball, particularly for the youth of Cayman. The two-week annual Esso Basketball coaching camp is a highlight of the summer calendar. In the arts field, Esso is a contributor to the National Cayman Islands Museum, National Trust and the National Art Gallery and was a major donor to the Maritime Heritage Foundation's Memorial Statue in honour of Caymanians who lost their lives at sea.

The important role Esso, its service stations and dealers play in the Cayman community was epitomised in the response following Hurricane Ivan to keep the island moving and assist the community. For example the company delivered fuel to the hospital and hurricane shelters, and donated significant funds to purchase medical supplies.

Esso's commitment to protecting the environment comes with a pledge to operate flawlessly in everything it does and to invest in the latest environmental fuel installations in service stations, ship and pipeline operations, and road haulage. The company looks forward to a further 70 years of flawless operation, supplying high-quality petroleum products and delivering excellent service to the Cayman Islands' community.

'Catch of the Day', featuring Country and Western star Bob Moseley

Skateboarding at Grand Harbour

DISTRICT OF GEORGE TOWN

Cayman Rugby Football Club

Musicians at the Cayfest Arts Festival

Spicy jerk chicken, a Cayman speciality

Butterfield Bank's annual 5K Irish Jog

Buying flowers at Every Bloomin' Thing

The Conch House

Butterfly Farm

A young butterfly lover

Sea, sand and sunshine

Poised for exciting development

There are probably few places on the planet where it is possible to send or receive mail from Hell. But in Grand Cayman, there is a place called Hell and the Post Office operates a facility there.

The Hell Post Office is perhaps one of the more unique aspects of postal operations in the Cayman Islands and has inspired a wide range of strange things. For instance, it once featured as the subject of a Sunday School lesson for children overseas who had written down a number of sins – which they then mailed to the office for symbolic destruction in hell.

The story of early postal development in the

Postcard from Hell!

Islands is closely linked to their administration under Jamaica and their seafaring history. As most men earned a living at sea, the post was a vital link between them and their loved ones back home. It was the means of sending money home to family as well as sending and receiving news of friends and relatives. Residents greeted the arrival of ships with enthusiasm as much for the supplies they brought as for the mail they carried. Mail was often sent home via Jamaica. Today, its delivery is no longer limited to

The General Post Office, under the watchful eye of a Blue Iguana

Mail from the world

transit through Jamaica but arrives directly from a number of different countries.

The Cayman Islands Post Office operates 15 post offices and two postal agencies throughout all three islands. Mail is delivered primarily via private letter boxes. There is no home delivery of mail, but this is a culturally accepted norm for Caymanians who, for decades, have been accustomed to going to a local post office to collect their mail.

Delivery to private letter boxes has not hampered service significantly. In fact, the quality of postal services has played a quiet but important role in the development of the country's financial sector. The Cayman Islands Post Office is now handling more than 10 million pieces of letter, registered, parcel and Express Mail Service items for the less than 50,000 residents and citizens. Given the small population and high volume of mail, residents in turn enjoy a high per capita mail service.

In 1997, the Airport

Philatelic Bureau collectibles

Postal Union's Express Mail Service (EMS) Cooperative. For the past couple of years, the Cayman Islands has ranked in the top 20 countries that comprise the cooperative and rose as high as number nine overall in 2003 rankings.

As part of the commitment to quality service under the EMS Cooperative, there is a limited delivery area in the capital, George Town, and the Seven Mile Beach area on Grand Cayman. In so doing, the Post Office is able to offer local delivery of the majority of EMS items that arrive from overseas.

In recent years, there has been investment in upgrading the Islands'

five to seven commemorative stamp issues are released. In addition to stamps, first-day covers and souvenir sheets are also produced for sale. From time to time, special collector items are created for particular stamp issues.

The Cayman Islands Post Office is poised on the threshold of an exciting future. Innovations in technology are expected to bring growth in new e-commerce products and services. Growth is also expected in the parcel sector and from the development of the Islands' philatelic products.

Express delivery

Sorting the mail

Post Office and Mail Processing Centre was opened. This facility introduced computerised mail dispatching, as well as track and trace services for the registered, parcel and Express mailstreams. However, the majority of the mailsorting operations are still on manual systems. The Post Office is a member of the Universal

postal facilities infrastructure. This has laid the foundation for the next stage of development, to better meet the 21st-century needs of the Islands' customers. These new developments are expected to help the Post Office become more commercially driven, as it takes advantage of various e-business opportunities to create new products and services.

Cayman Islands stamps are well known and valued by collectors for their high quality. The Philatelic Bureau oversees the production and release process for the country's definitive and commemorative stamp issues. Themes are first and foremost of local interest and culture, but also include British royalty and the commemoration of international anniversaries and events.

A 12-stamp definitive issue is released every five years. Each year, between

Ann James, PMG Sheena Glasgow and Melissa Martinez-Ebanks

Parcel post operations

A perfect destination

By The Cayman Islands Department of Tourism

The stark beauty of The Bluff in Cayman Brac

The Cayman Islands is made up of a trio of islands located 480 miles (770 km) south-west of Miami, with a population of approximately 40,000. All three are very different. Grand Cayman, home to the capital George Town, is the largest. Cayman Brac, the second largest, has spectacular scenery and fantastic wildlife and diving. Little Cayman is a tiny paradise island, where visitors land on a dirt air strip and are more likely to come across the island's indigenous iguanas crossing the roads than another vehicle or one of the island's bicycles, which are commonly used to get around.

The Cayman Islands stands out as having some of the best diving in the Caribbean and is generally considered to be one of the world's top three snorkelling destinations. With over 300 dive and snorkel sites between the three islands, divers enjoy spectacular underwater visibility of up to 30 metres and temperatures of around 80°F (27°C). The geography of the islands enables divers to experience some of the best wall diving in the world, not to mention innumerable fascinating

shipwrecks. The drop-offs, such as the Bloody Bay Wall in Little Cayman and the Cayman Wall in Cayman Brac, are rated some of the finest on Earth. All the diving is relatively close to the shore, generally within a 15-minute boat ride, largely because the Cayman Islands are in fact the top of a submerged mountain range. All levels of diving courses are available, including resort courses, full-certification courses, open-water referral dives and most internationally recognised instruction courses. More than 30 self-regulated operators provide diving services on all three islands.

With the underwater world also easily accessible to snorkellers, one of the most popular and remarkable underwater attractions for visitors is Stingray City, where depths vary from one to four metres. Here it is possible to swim with more than 100 stingrays, who love to interact with their two-legged visitors. A variety of submersibles also provide more than a close-up glimpse of marine life for those who would rather stay dry, including a

A favourite diving destination

three-man sub that can transport visitors down through depths up to 1,000 feet (305 m), where marine life looks virtually prehistoric.

The Cayman Islands also has much to offer visitors above the sea, with attractions such as the Cayman Turtle Farm, the Queen Elizabeth II Botanic Park, Pedro St. James 'Castle' and Rum Point. For those wishing to simply relax and swim in the sunshine, there are few places with greater appeal than famous Seven Mile Beach. Good restaurants also abound throughout the islands, offering local cuisine and international food. Accommodation ranges from budget self-catering apartments to the luxury of the five-star resorts.

Cayman's tourist attractions serve not just to extend its appeal to visitors, but also to preserve, protect and restore the islands' national heritage and treasures. Cayman has a fascinating history

Away from it all in Little Cayman

Queen Elizabeth II Botanic Park

A shopper's paradise

where visitors can swim with turtles, the Predator Tank and the Aviary and Iguana Sanctuary.

Both Little Cayman and Cayman Brac – Grand Cayman's Sister Islands – are a short flight away from Grand Cayman and make a perfect escape for visitors seeking a quieter taste of life during their Caymanian holiday. These islands offer a variety of accommodation and several restaurants.

With tourism such an integral part of Cayman Islands life, it is no surprise that the industry provides thousands of jobs locally. Because there are too many jobs to be filled by the local population, many people come from overseas on work permits, drawn by the appeal of the island life, year-round good climate and high standard of living. The tourism sector supplies thousands of jobs in the hotel and accommodation field, from managerial positions down, as well as in the water sports industry, from dive instructors to submarine pilots. Overall, tourism contributes hundreds of millions of dollars to the local economy each year and it is estimated

and 2003 was Quincentennial Year, marking the first 500 years of its recorded history. Christopher Columbus first discovered the Cayman Islands in 1503, naming them 'Las Tortugas' (after the islands' abundant turtles), later to be renamed as the Cayman Islands. Festivals, carnivals and displays were organised all year round to mark the anniversary.

In the wake of Hurricane Ivan, which swept through the Caribbean in September 2004, the Cayman Islands is set to reap the rewards of a considerable investment programme. This investment will take it to the very top of the league table of Caribbean tourist destinations. Grand Cayman already has an enviable portfolio of quality accommodation. This ranges from the six-star luxury of the new flagship Ritz-Carlton Grand Cayman on Seven Mile Beach to all-suite hotels, condominiums, dive lodges, budget properties and local B&Bs – all of which share with guests the warm hospitality and welcome that is so typical of the Caymanian people.

One of the island's most popular tourist attractions, the Turtle Farm, has also expanded with the development of Boatswain's Beach, a new 30-acre multi-million pound marine theme park. Uniquely Caymanian in its design, the park combines a state-of-the-art research facility for the conservation of sea turtles with attractions such as Saltwater Snorkel Lagoon,

The unique Blue Iguana

that over 50% of GDP and 75% of foreign currency earnings are generated from this industry.

Promoting the destination to international visitors falls to the Cayman Islands Department of Tourism. The organisation celebrated the fruits of its labours when visitors topped the one-million visitor milestone in 1995. The tourism industry has continued to flourish since, with over 2.1 million visitors annually, of which some 300,000 arrive by air and the remainder by cruise ship. The United States market provides the largest number of tourists, with Europe and Canada vying for second place. Both the US and Canadian markets tend to be largely

seasonal and shorter stay in nature. The United Kingdom and European countries provide a complementary balance, with year-round visits and longer stays.

As well as being one of the Caribbean's top beach and dive destinations, the Cayman Islands is proving to be a big draw for the lucrative wedding and honeymoon market. Cayman has an abundance of romantic locations and accommodation options to choose from, and a fabulous array of activities to suit most couples seeking the holiday of a lifetime with beach and adventure rolled into one. Grand Cayman has a large number of specialist wedding organisers and professionals, who have recognised that most couples need to be treated with a high degree of individuality and require tailor-made, personalised weddings and honeymoons.

The special-interest market – such as wildlife and birdwatching – is also growing significantly. Cayman Brac in particular has a unique appeal for those prepared to travel for their hobby.

Cayman also lends itself to the conference and incentive market, thanks to the wide range of hotel and resort accommodation on offer and the diversity of leisure activities. With direct flights from the UK four times a week and easy access from the US, the excellent infrastructure and professionalism of the local hotel and leisure industry make Grand Cayman a highly desirable destination for conference organisers seeking to add more than a touch of paradise to any business event.

Vacation time

Bars and restaurants abound

BATABANO
Carnival

and energy to the company. He soon realised he had a talent for marketing, development and promotion. Expansion on products carrying the Tortuga name was underway. Following the introduction of the Tortuga Gold and Light rums came over a dozen more varieties of Tortuga rums.

Not content to stop there, he developed a line of Tortuga private label gourmet food products consisting of rum fudge, a variety of Caribbean sauces (one of which – Tortuga Hell Fire Sauce – is a Scovie Fiery Foods Award Winner), Rum Punch Mix, Chocolate & Plain Rum mints, gourmet coffees, syrups, Chocolate Hazelnut Rum Truffles, Pepper Jelly, Tortuga Honey's and the addition of more flavours of the now 'World Famous Tortuga Rum Cake'.

Tortuga is now a global name. The company's office and distribution centre in Miami, Florida handles the constantly growing year-round mail order business and services thousands of repeat customers worldwide. It also launched a complete cyberspace store on its secure

The essence of success

December 15th, 1984 was the day husband and wife team Robert and Carlene Hamaty formed a little company in Grand Cayman. They called it 'Tortuga Rum Company', deriving the name from the original one given to the Cayman Islands, Las Tortugas, meaning 'The Turtles'.

They started their company with the introduction of two rums, Tortuga Gold and Tortuga Light Rum, blended and bottled exclusively for the newly formed company. Both Robert and Carlene were still employed by Cayman Airways, he as a chief pilot and Carlene as an in-flight supervisor.

It was at this time that Carlene started baking rum cakes in her own kitchen using an old family recipe that had been given to her by her mother. She sold these cakes to local restaurants to feature as their dessert item. She of course used Tortuga Gold Rum.

Today, Tortuga Rum Company headquarters is a 10,000 square foot, state-of-the-art bakery producing in excess of 10,000 rum cakes a day, all from the same secret recipe that has been handed down through Carlene's family for generations. Each freshly baked cake is hand-glazed with a specially blended premium oak barrel-aged five-year old Tortuga Gold Rum. Sophisticated vacuum packing machines ensure the cakes have a shelf life of six months or more, and will last indefinitely if refrigerated or frozen. They are then heat sealed and boxed for shipping locally and worldwide. Tortuga Rum cakes are available in three sizes: 33oz. large, 16oz. medium and 4oz. mini.

Soon after the company's launch, the couple

Company founder Robert Hamaty

acquired their first 'Tortuga Duty Free Liquors' store on the waterfront in George Town. This enabled them to service the thousands of cruise ship passengers that arrived daily. In a short period of time, four more duty free liquor shops were opened, followed by airport duty free stores and several Tortuga Liquor's Fines Wines & Spirits stores. Over a 20-year period, Tortuga Rum Company would grow to include 17 locations in all.

In 1991 Robert was struck with a virus that affected the muscles of his heart, resulting in a heart transplant. In February 1996, he received the heart of a 27-year old pilot who had died in a skydiving accident. The profession of the donor was especially uncanny given Robert's long and impressive career as a pilot himself. After a six-month recovery period, he devoted all his time

website. Shoppers can now order 24-hours a day from lively colourful photographs with detailed descriptions of all the Tortuga gourmet products available for shipping.

Robert and Carlene Hamaty have dedicated a tremendous amount of time and effort to creating their company. They are proud to admit to being the first company to produce rum cake not only in the Cayman Islands but throughout the Caribbean, as well as with their franchises in Jamaica, Bahamas and Barbados. Credited with being one of the pioneers of developing a global awareness of Caribbean fancy food items, the couple has been rewarded with unsolicited recognition from prestigious television shows and numerous television and radio gourmet food shows around the world. The most recent honour to be bestowed on Robert was a 'Caribbean Entrepreneur of the Year' award.

From its inception 20 years ago, Tortuga Rum Company Ltd. has grown to become the largest duty free liquor business in the Cayman Islands. The name has also become synonymous with one of the world's finest confections: the authentic and original Tortuga Rum Cake – the Cayman Islands' number one export and souvenir item. Truly the sweet smell of success!

The headquarters and bakery of the Tortuga Rum Company Limited

The Caribbean high flyer

Cayman Airways has been the national flag carrier of the Cayman Islands since 1968. The dynamic airline with the turtle logo flies scheduled services to the United States, Jamaica and Cuba, in addition to operating multiple regular flights within the Islands themselves.

The airline's initial flights linked Grand Cayman with its sister islands of Cayman Brac and Little Cayman. Within four years it was flying further afield, shuttling passengers to and from Miami in the US.

In 1978 the 'Sir Turtle' logo was adopted, in recognition of the Islands' best-known native inhabitant. A second US route, to Houston, was also launched that year.

Services were significantly expanded in the 1980s, with charter operations to 11 cities in the United States. Three of them – Tampa, Atlanta and New York – were turned into non-stop scheduled service routes. By 1989, to keep pace with growing passenger numbers, the fleet had been upgraded to include larger aircraft in the form of the Boeing 737-400.

Airlines the world over experienced a business downturn in the early 1990s. This, together with increased competition on the Miami route and an oil crisis, obliged Cayman Airways to restructure, leading to fewer plane numbers and the elimination of first class.

By the late 1990s, the situation had improved and the airline grew again. Several years later it faced the global negative impact of 9/11 and underwent a short period of retrenchment and service cutbacks in 2002. However, the airline soon bounced back with a programme of modest and controlled schedule expansion. It also introduced consumer-friendly price reductions and made improvements to customer service that resulted in a resurgence of air travel to/from the Cayman Islands and an upsurge in tourism arrivals.

Today the company operates a fleet of seven aircraft. This includes three Boeing 737-200 jets, one of which is a cargo freighter, two Boeing 737-300s and two Twin Otter turboprops. Together these aircraft serve ten points in the US and Caribbean all year-round. The US gateways include Miami, Fort Lauderdale, Tampa, Houston and Chicago, with regional connections to Cayman Brac and Little Cayman, the Cuban capital Havana, and Montego Bay and Kingston in Jamaica. In addition, seasonal summer service is offered to Orlando, Florida.

In response to market demand, the airline recently began seasonal service to its seventh US gateway – Boston, Massachusetts. It also provides express service through frequent daily flights to and from Cayman Brac and Little Cayman with the Twin Otter turboprops, which are ideal for the short take-offs and landings on the airstrips of these two islands.

As a multinational carrier, Cayman Airways meets the safety regulations of three separate aviation entities. They are the United Kingdom's Civil Aviation Authority, the Federal Aviation Authority in the US and the CAA of the Cayman Islands.

The airline's frequent flyer programme, Sir Turtle Rewards, features three award levels and is designed so that passengers can earn rewards faster than with almost any other airline. For air-cargo shipments, the airline offers three types of service – General Cargo, Guaranteed Priority and JIFFY. Depending on the shipment's urgency, the size of the items being shipped and other factors, customers can choose the method of shipment which best meets their needs.

Whether travelling inter-Island or to/from one of its gateway cities, Cayman Airways strives to provide passengers with the unique personalised service of a small-island airline with world-class credentials.

Seven Mile Beach

Something for everybody

Margarita time!

The warm Caribbean waters

Topping up the tan

Making a new friend

Encircled

Jack and Todd at Calico Jack's

Beach-front condominiums

Seven Mile Beach

A stroll along the shore

A smile says it all

A day at the beach

Enjoying the sun

A beautiful Cayman sunset

Coconut Joe's

The Jolly Roger

An opportune moment for investment

By Kim Lund, Broker/Owner, RE/MAX Cayman Islands

As we enter the last half of this decade, property values in the Cayman Islands are starting to take off and should gather speed for the next several years. Over the last five years, the real estate market has fallen asleep because of limited development activity and falling air-arrival tourism. It is now way behind the curve, but is beginning a phase of rapid capital appreciation as tourism is being aggressively promoted and accelerates. At the same time, development activity has risen to a fever pitch.

Traditionally, the Cayman Islands' real estate market has risen in steps. During the early part of each decade, the market tends to be flat. From the middle of the decade onwards, demand for property and its prices boom. The same scenario is being played out this decade, but on a much larger scale than seen in the past, as the Cayman Islands enter a period of rapid growth.

Most of the investment is focused on Grand Cayman, which is the location of the Islands' government, financial industry and most of their tourism. The attraction is a well-developed infrastructure, safe environment, no currency restrictions, political stability and a ranking as the fifth-largest financial centre in the world. Equally important are Seven Mile Beach and the clear warm Caribbean Sea. The Cayman Islands are rated as having some of the world's best beaches and diving destinations.

The Islands are currently experiencing a rapid expansion of their financial industry and tourism infrastructure, their economy's twin pillars. As a result of this growth, both demand for property and development activity have increased significantly. Yet the supply is extremely limited because of a slowdown in development during the first half of the decade and a major hurricane that destroyed and damaged many homes and buildings in 2004. Adding fuel to the fire is the explosive growth the Islands are currently experiencing in financial and tourism business.

These factors have set the stage for a potential appreciation of anywhere from 25% to 100% or more in the next five years. Still, in some unique cases, properties are selling for around what it would cost to buy the land and build. This is creating a multitude of opportunities for investors, but they are now being snapped up quickly.

New development in George Town, the business and commercial capital, is on the rise. Cruise ship business has more than doubled in the last five years. With the financial industry now on

Cayman Islands Yacht Club

Beautiful home at The Shores, West Bay

An attractive North Side residence

114

Regal Beach Club

Beach-front condominiums

Charming family house close to Cayman Kai

Elegant family residence

the rebound, new seven-storey buildings are being planned (five storeys was the highest previously), the first of which is for Bank of Butterfield. Hurricane Ivan destroyed and damaged a few George Town buildings, such as the government's Tower Building, which will likely be sold and redeveloped. There is a continuing trend to redevelop the older bank buildings in prime locations and the Cayman National Bank building is next in line for development into retail shops, restaurants and offices.

Mega resorts and developments are being built, introducing a new and affluent clientele to the real estate market. The Ritz-Carlton Resort is to open a 365-suite beach-front and inland property, followed by villas and homes around the resort's Greg Norman-designed golf course and marina. Other resorts, such as the Mandarin Oriental with its 114-suite boutique hotel, will be developing a presence in Grand Cayman. A 240-acre world-class commercial and residential development incorporating Venetian-style canals is now under construction and in its first phase. Another, yet unnamed, hotel and condominium development of approximately 400 acres is preparing to announce its plan to start construction.

Several new condominium developments are breaking ground along Seven Mile Beach. In most cases, this new wave of development is replacing older properties, which are being torn down and redeveloped. Some of these were planned before the hurricane struck, but others have come afterwards. Prices for prime beach-front properties, either new construction or resales, range from approximately US$650,000 for a two-bedroom condominium to US$6 million or more for four-bedroom penthouses. A 20,000-square foot penthouse condominium residence at the Ritz-Carlton is on the market for US$40 million.

Along Seven Mile Beach, there are currently five new condominium developments under construction or ready to start. These include Water's Edge, Caribbean Club, Renaissance, Montclaire and Beachcomber. Other Seven Mile Beach developments are being contemplated, especially in light of the pre-construction sales success of these projects. However, the difficulty for new construction is the lack of available beach-front land for hotel and condominium development. This will keep the amount of new condominiums in short supply and prices increasing, as construction slows after this current wave of development is completed.

Beach-front and sea-front homes are another sought-after type of resort property. The hurricane destroyed or damaged a significant percentage of these properties, so there is an extremely short supply on the market. This has created opportunities for new construction, as well as improvements to existing properties that were damaged but are being repaired. There have only been two recorded hurricanes, since 1900, to hit the Cayman Islands with winds over 100 miles (160 kilometres) per hour. So Hurricane Ivan in 2004 is being viewed as an anomaly.

The local real estate market is just starting to ramp up. There is no better time to invest and reap the rewards that a buoyant market can afford and, as an investment, there is precious little that will match the returns of Cayman Islands' real estate over the next several years.

Pinnacle Condominiums, Seven Mile Beach

For Sale
Shown by appointment only
4 BED + BONUS
ROOM, 4.5 BATH, CUSTOM
BUILT, 6,000 SQ. FT.; BOAT SLIP,
POOL, BRAND NEW!

RE/MAX
CAYMAN ISLANDS
KIM LUND
916-5555
949-9772
CIREBA MEMBER

RE/MAX owner Kim Lund with clients

The property professionals

As early as the 1980s, there was little more than commercial and residential real estate available in the Cayman Islands. However, their real estate market has become far more complex over the last 25 years, evolving into a burgeoning and multifaceted industry.

Since 1990, when RE/MAX Cayman Islands was founded by Broker/Owner Kim Douglas Lund, the company has been positioned to grow with the market. Its Associates specialise in all the various fields within the real estate industry – among them beach-front condominiums and homes, commercial, new developments, land, bank foreclosures and industrial.

The company is an independently owned and operated franchise of RE/MAX International, which has affiliated offices in 55 countries worldwide and over 100,000 Brokers and Associates. Within the Cayman Islands office, Mr Lund has set up his own 'Lund Team' to focus on the handling of customer service, communication and response time. This team consists of a core group of the most experienced Associates and Administration personnel.

When asked about the advantage of a team approach, he says: "We work exclusively with overseas investors and clients. We need to provide regular, consistent communication and market updates, not to mention an immediate response to their inquiries. By having my own team within the office, we are able to be much more responsive. Since we all work together as a cohesive team, any of us can respond to queries, instead of waiting for one particular person to be available."

From an experience standpoint, it does not get much better than this for real estate. Mr Lund has lived in the Cayman Islands since 1984 and has over two decades' experience in the local market for property management and real estate. As a 'top producer', he has received the highest awards possible from RE/MAX International. These include being number one worldwide for two consecutive years and being a member of the Circle of Legends, of which there are only 38 members within the whole RE/MAX organisation.

During his career in real estate, Mr Lund has built an enviable reputation. He works in this market on a daily basis and is actively involved in every transaction that his team procures. Asked why he chose this extremely hectic lifestyle, he replies: "Real estate has always been a passion for me and I would never consider leaving this business. It is in my blood and I enjoy every aspect of it." His success speaks for itself.

Investors considering a real estate purchase in the Cayman Islands need proper representation. This can only be achieved by someone with the experience, contacts and local knowledge to make the investment process as smooth and problem-free as possible. Mr Lund and his 'Lund Team' have those credentials and a very long list of loyal clients. Considering the importance and size of real estate investments, it makes sense to work with the best. The cost of not doing so can be enormous.

Magnificent canal-front residence

Strand Shopping Centre

The Great House on Seven Mile Beach

The Islands' driving force

Cico Avis Car Rentals has been successfully serving the Cayman Islands for some four decades. Renowned for its quality and attention to detail, the company offers the Islands' largest range of cars and is the sole rental firm to have offices in all the nation's major hotels.

David and Steve Foster established Cico Rent-A-Car in 1966. The two brothers sought to build a business with the highest standard of customer care and service. Their ambition soon paid dividends, creating the Islands' premier car-rental company. Today it is an Avis International affiliate and strictly adheres to Avis monthly quality-assurance programmes and services.

Through its rental office locations, the company consistently offers competitive and affordable rates and special discounts to groups and repeat customers. Further savings are available to clients who pre-book their vehicle on-line. The company's website provides detailed information on these rates as well as its extensive fleet of quality vehicles.

The firm also works exclusively with many of the cruise ship companies that drop anchor off George Town, offering passengers special one-day car-hire packages. They have the choice of two rental packages.

Cruise ship passengers arriving in George Town also benefit from the Avis courtesy pickup, located at the Blue Iguana souvenir shop, on the waterfront close to the South Passenger Terminal. From there they are quickly transported to the company's main rental office, just minutes away. A courtesy ride back to the port is also available, following the rental cars' return.

The company currently has five locations. In addition to the head office adjacent to Owen Roberts International Airport, it has offices conveniently situated at the Hyatt Regency, Westin Casuarina, Marriott Beach Resort and Courtyard Marriott. Clients may pick up their vehicles or can return them to any of these company locations.

The company's fleet consists of a wide selection of dependable, popular and exciting automobiles. They include compact cars, such as the Daihatsu Cuore, through to mid-sized models by Honda, Ford and Chrysler, not to mention convertibles and the very latest Jeeps. Top of the range is the Ford Expedition - Premium SUV, which can seat up to nine people. All the firm's vehicles are less than twelve months old, equipped to high specifications and feature air conditioning.

Company founders David and Steve Foster

Whether visiting Grand Cayman as a leisure traveller or on business, clients of Cico Avis may rest assured they will be offered a specifically tailored package. Once behind the wheel, they are free to explore the highways and byways in the comfort and style one would expect of the Cayman Islands' leading car rental company.

Grand Cayman's leading luxury hotel

Just outside and below the window, the surf laps restfully at the shore. Across the azure waters, the gentle waves roll onto the beach, hardly disturbing a grain of the dazzling powder-white sand that stretches for miles in either direction. This must be where the ocean comes for a vacation, an onlooker would surely decide, while scanning the fabled Seven Mile Beach of Grand Cayman Island, jewel of the Caribbean.

Both the lagoon and the island teem with life – colourful, exotic, yet so approachable. Visitors will struggle to decide whether to grab their fins and glide along the vibrant coral reef – home to over 168 memorable dive sites – or swim with the menacing-looking yet peaceful residents of Stingray City. At the end of the day, they can simply settle back in a beach chair to enjoy the rhythmic rustling of the palm trees while awaiting a truly world-class sunset.

This private paradise is just outside guests' door at the newly renovated Grand Cayman Marriott Beach Resort. Located where the world-famous Seven Mile Beach begins, the resort received the prestigious 2004 World Travel Award, naming it 'Grand Cayman's Leading Hotel'.

Designed to be an integral part of the true island experience, the resort is an enchanting collage of lush tropical landscaping, classic Cayman furnishings, and soft hues of sea and sun, sky and sand. It soon becomes difficult to tell where the hotel ends and the island begins.

The resort's newly remodelled rooms are some of the island's most spacious, offering superb sea views from their balcony. Inside each of the 307 guestrooms, guests are surrounded by rich hues of gold, tangerine and avocado mixed elegantly with dark woods and artful appointments. Rooms come with a plush lounge chair, a large marbled bathroom, and luxurious fresh linen for the king-size bed or two double beds. Guest amenities include an in-room safe, mini refrigerator, cable TV, coffee-maker, hairdryer, iron with full-size ironing board, as well as high-speed Internet access.

The Grand Cayman Marriott Beach Resort is the closest full-service hotel to the bustling harbour town of George Town. The resort's staff can arrange for a bicycle, scooter or car rental at competitive prices – though the resort is in fact conveniently situated for walking to many nearby sights and attractions.

Ocean activities available from the resort's beach include sailing, deep-sea fishing, parasailing, snorkelling and scuba diving. Famous as one of the world's best dive areas, the sea and coral reefs surrounding Grand Cayman abound with exotic and colourful tropical fish. Friendly dive shops can be found throughout the island. However, the resort has its very own dive shop, at Red Sail Sports, where the professional staff are always on hand to help guests eager to explore the magic of the sea.

The resort has a wide selection of dining facilities. The Red Parrot, which seats 100 comfortably, is open throughout the day and features a classically comfortable setting. It is rich in hues of bright Caribbean colour mixed elegantly with dark woods and local art. Guests may start their day with a full breakfast buffet including fresh tropical fruit, traditional breakfast fare or tempting made-to-order dishes. The Steak & Sea-food Bistro menu is designed to be an artistic statement of Caribbean fusion. Lunch-time specialties include creamed conch chowder with green banana spoons, while the

irresistible international gourmet alfresco dining with a Caribbean flair, carefully composed by the resort's award-winning chefs. Lunch here is a casual affair, ranging from toasted ham and Brie panini to the chef's island-famous jerked calamari.

As the sun begins to set over the sea, dinner at Solana begins with the award-winning Cayman turtle fritters served with a spicy papaya chutney. Tempting main-course dishes include cab tenderloin on spirilli onions with white asparagus and Boursin Jus. Guests can round off their meal with Ron's Mudslide madness – an inimitable frozen creation.

At the resort's La Mer Spa, which proudly introduces YonKa therapy, guests are invited to abandon their worldly cares and allow qualified professionals to pamper them in style. This exquisite, world-renowned skin-care line is based on aromatherapy, fruit therapy and marine therapy. International therapists and stylists are on hand to help guests choose

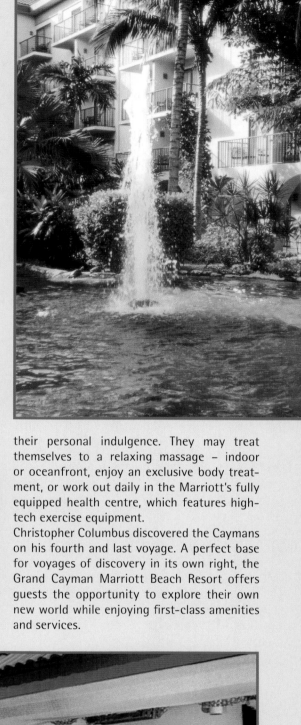

dinner menu offers island-inspired entrees such as Adobo spiny lobster atop a jasmine rice cake with fused annato butter.

Balboa's Lounge, in the resort's centre lobby, is the heart of the hotel's activity. Local artists, musicians and even cigar-rollers bring the island culture right into the hotel for guests' enjoyment. The lounge is a full bar, offering tapas, speciality Martinis (over a 100 varieties so far!) and light meals daily. In the evening, guests can also enjoy a Cognac, Armagnac or other fine liqueurs while listening to the island's best live music.

Sol Bar is located on the resort's pristine beachfront overlooking the Caribbean Sea. It is a perfect spot for relaxing and enjoying a cool tropical cocktail and lunch. It offers a complete lunch menu, but its famous Beach BBQ is a favourite with hotel guests and islanders alike. As the sun starts to set over the ocean, Sol Bar comes alive with Caribbean music and some of the best island-inspired tropical drinks on Grand Cayman. As the stars come out over the beach and the sea, guests can enjoy an after-dinner drink from an extensive list of superior wines, brandies and liquors from the Marriott's own cellar.

Solana on Seven Mile Beach is the Marriott's four-star ocean-front restaurant. Elegant and intimate, it features one of the finest wine selections on the island. The Solana offers seating for up to 120 diners. A professional special event team is also on hand to organise special occasions ranging from intimate romantic dinners to weddings, business meetings, functions and parties.

Inspired by the art, culture and cuisine of the Caribbean, Chef Ron Hargrave welcomes guests with the finest dining experience in Grand Cayman. Solana delights the senses with the aroma of local spices, the sounds of the sea, tastes that inspire and the sight of the island's breathtaking sunsets. While relaxing under the open-air canopy, guests are treated to

their personal indulgence. They may treat themselves to a relaxing massage – indoor or oceanfront, enjoy an exclusive body treatment, or work out daily in the Marriott's fully equipped health centre, which features high-tech exercise equipment.

Christopher Columbus discovered the Caymans on his fourth and last voyage. A perfect base for voyages of discovery in its own right, the Grand Cayman Marriott Beach Resort offers guests the opportunity to explore their own new world while enjoying first-class amenities and services.

Seven Wonders on Seven Mile Beach

An era of unparalleled luxury and elegance is being ushered in with The Ritz-Carlton, Grand Cayman and its exclusive collection of spacious ocean-front homes known as The Residences. Situated on 144 acres of prime real estate stretching from Seven Mile Beach to the North Sound, this US$500 million resort is the island's most prestigious new development.

In total, the resort offers 365 guest rooms and 69 private oceanfront homes. It also features Cayman's largest ballroom, a luxury shopping emporium with premium brands, five restaurants and a host of watersports. Yet what sets this resort apart from any other – besides its inspired personal service – is the extraordinary array of facilities and activities on offer. They include a spa, restaurants, tennis courts, golf course and children's programme created by renowned experts in their field.

Known as 'The Seven Wonders on Seven Mile Beach', these activities and facilities set a gold standard for Grand Cayman's resorts. The first of these wonders is the gracious service of over 1,000 ladies and gentlemen of The Ritz-Carlton, all committed to providing genuine care and comfort to each guest and Residence owner. Furthermore, guests and owners can tap into a range of one-of-a-kind experiences that only this resort can offer.

Second of the wonders is Blue Tip, a world-class golf course designed by the renowned Australian professional Greg Norman. Carved along serpentine waterways with sweeping views of the North Sound, the 120-acre course

has water features on eight holes and demands a dramatic finish with an island green on number nine.

Wonder number three comprises several restaurants bearing the name of Eric Ripert, the executive chef and co-owner of New York's top-rated Le Bernardin. Blue by Eric Ripert is a must for aficionados of the freshest and

most delicious fish dishes, while Periwinkle by Eric Ripert is a lively al fresco grill restaurant imbued with his Mediterranean heritage.

The spa by La Prairie, Switzerland is managed by the leader in Swiss skincare and European spa treatments. The fourth of the resort's wonders, this establishment achieves a perfect fusion of skincare with the art of beauty. The 20,000 square foot, 17-treatment room spa is also Cayman's largest and most luxurious. La Prairie hand-picked The Ritz-Carlton, Grand Cayman as the home of its first Caribbean spa and its first to be inspired by the company's exclusive fragrance Silver Rain.

Ambassadors of the Environment by Jean-Michel Cousteau, wonder number five, is a children's programme put together by the man renowned around the globe for his exploration and preservation activities. The programme enables young resort guests to reconnect with nature by taking part in ecological adventures that introduce them to Cayman's reefs, mangroves, woodlands, wildlife and cultural heritage. They can also engage in a range of sports – among them snorkelling, kayaking and hiking – or activities such as creating multimedia presentations with digital imaging.

Tennis by Nick Bollettieri is a customised

programme put together by The Ritz-Carlton, Grand Cayman and the world's most famous tennis coach. The brand-new facilities at this tennis centre – which has no equal in the Caribbean – include The Courts, offering three red clay courts and one grass court, staffed by professionals trained by Bollettieri. Resort guests can also receive instruction from the great man himself through the centre's interactive video coaching facilities.

Exclusivity by The Reserve is the name of the resort's seventh and final wonder. Guests staying here – at any of the 24 two-to-three bedroom condominiums with views over Seven Mile Beach – need not choose between the service and facilities of a world-class resort and the comfort of a private ocean-front home. For they benefit fully from enhancements to the resort's already high service, including a dedicated concierge, butler service, separate check-in area and access to The Observatory, a private terrace and Cayman's highest point for stargazing and admiring sunsets.

The only experience to surpass a stay at The Ritz-Carlton, Grand Cayman is owning one of the 69 private ocean-front homes located on the property. Situated directly on Seven Mile Beach, The Residences are offered in two, three or six-bedroom floor plans (2,400-20,000 square feet), each with open-floor designs, nine to 12-foot ceilings, the finest finishes, and the highest quality appliances and fixtures. Each Residence has a professionally equipped chef's kitchen and multiple terraces overlooking the Caribbean Sea.

The Residences also include Endless Service, an exclusive collection of personalised services, interior design, furniture, luxury automobiles

and boats which cannot be found elsewhere in the Caribbean. For example, while in residence, home-owners have a BMW at their disposal and access to a fleet of crewed powerboats. They are also offered privileged access to all resort facilities, including two lifetime memberships to the Blue Tip golf course. Owners also enjoy around-the-clock attention from a residential concierge team, valet parking and security, private entrances and elevators.

With its luxury accommodation, unique dining and superior leisure facilities, The Ritz-Carlton, Grand Cayman is raising the Caribbean tourism experience to previously unmatched levels. Those standards are poised to continue rising, as the resort is soon to include 200 golf-course villas, a marina for large yachts and marina residences overlooking the North Sound.

The Grand Caymanian Resort

Grand Cayman's Premier Vacation Ownership Resort

The Grand Caymanian Resort promises a world-class vacation in one of the world's most beautiful destinations. Luxury, convenience and fun are the hallmark of this exclusive resort, which is adjacent to The Links Championship Golf Course at Safe-haven, Grand Cayman. It is also the first and only resort to grace the shores of the island's majestic North Sound.

One of the Caribbean's premier vacation ownership clubs, the award-winning resort is proud of its Five Star Rating from the highly respected timeshare vacation net-work Interval International. Membership opportunities are available on phase one in studio, one-bedroom and two-bedroom villas. The resort offers a 95-year lease and a flexible 'floating time' programme, guaranteeing its members the ultimate in choice and freedom.

The first phase of this outstanding resort comprises 54 villas, all enjoying ocean views. The resort is built in a British-Caribbean style and includes a freshwater swimming pool, large sun deck, whirl-pool, tennis court, beach volleyball court, an air-conditioned restaurant and bar, a dive and watersports sundry shop, not to mention concierge ser-vices. Parties, fun games and complimentary events are also organised on-site.

Fully furnished with all modern amenities for the convenience of guests, the villas offer two bedrooms, two bathrooms, terrace, full kitchen and a living-dining area. The guest bedroom can be locked-off and used independently of the rest of the villa and includes a small but comprehensively equipped kitchenette.

Those staying at the resort can enjoy a round or two at the adjacent Links Golf Course. Rated the best golf course in the Caribbean and the only 18-hole championship course

on Grand Cayman, it offers special prices for members and guests.

Making the most of its position by the North Sound, the resort provides a convenient, private boat dock with regular excursions to the world-famous Stingray City. One-stop watersports services, it is worth noting, are available on the property with Capt. Don's Cayman Diver Ltd. Conveniently located in the lobby, it offers first-class scuba diving on the exotic North Wall, snorkelling on beautiful North Sound reefs and deep-sea fishing. It caters to both

certified and beginner divers, while also offering tour desk services for activities off the resort. These include submarine tours, horseback riding excursions, helicopter rides, sunset sails, parasailing, fishing charters and pirate encounters.

The resort has always seen its members as its best form of advertising every time they travel and provides several great referral programmes and benefits. The 'friends and family' special, for example, allows members to send up to 10 guests a year to experience the resort for one week. Moreover, whenever a member refers a guest that joins, the resort will also pay their maintenance fee for one year.

Offering unequalled hospitality in the local tradition, The Grand Caymanian Resort succeeds in being a 'home away from home' for all its guests.

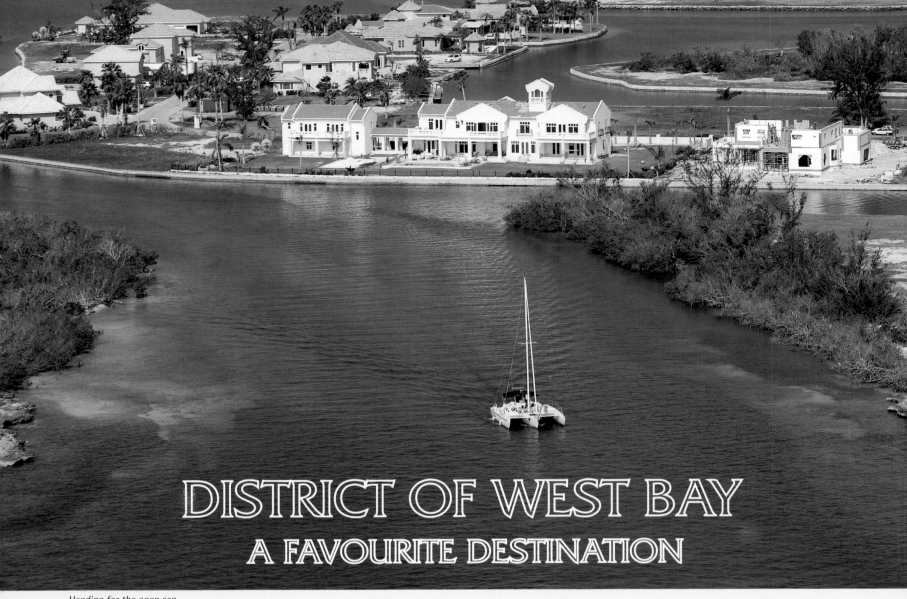

DISTRICT OF WEST BAY
A FAVOURITE DESTINATION

Heading for the open sea

West Bay is geographically the smallest and most concentrated of Grand Cayman's districts, but has the island's second largest population. It extends some six miles (9.7 km) northwards from the Westin Resort/Safehaven to Conch Point on the tip of the island's western peninsula. It was formerly known for its seafaring and matriarch-led families, and some of those strong bonds and extended family networks can still be seen here today.

West Bay includes a long stretch of the legendary Seven Mile Beach, a popular and highly developed tourist area that is not quite as long as its name suggests. For many holiday-makers, this is the place to enjoy the best that Cayman has to offer in terms of sun, sand and sea. It features idyllic beaches and crystal-clear seas for swimming and other watersports, as well as a host of restaurants, bars, shopping malls, hotels and condominiums lining West Bay Road all the way from the northern outskirts of George Town to Jackson's Pond. Just north of here is Cemetery Beach, a paradise for offshore snorkellers.

Before tourism took off in Cayman, this district was home to many of the island's mariners and turtlers. Its once-vital turtling industry produced vessels and crew of unparalleled quality, the latter referred to by modern historians and by nostalgic retirees as 'iron men and wooden ships'.

A trace of some of those memories is kept alive at the Cayman Turtle Farm, now part of the Boatswain's Beach marine theme park. Intended to be both educational and entertaining, the Turtle Farm is among Cayman's top visitor attractions. It has over 14,000 Green Sea Turtles as well as an active breeding and conservation programme for replenishing numbers that are endangered in the wild.

Not far away is the district's other main tourist attraction, the hamlet called Hell. The unique name likely originates from the appearance of

Traditional house on Boggy Sand Road

Looking towards George Town

Cayman Islands Yacht Club

District monument

Beautiful West Bay cottage

Cuban cigars, a popular purchase

the local jagged and black rocks, which could be taken for the brimstone of a very hot fire in hell. The gift shops make much capital of the place name and the tiny post office franks 'Hell, Grand Cayman' on the thousands of picture postcards mailed from here each year.

Less familiar but just as charming is Powell's Museum of Caymanian Heritage, containing a fascinating collection of local everyday artefacts and documents. The place was the brainchild of Tony Powell, who opened his museum in an old general store.

The district has managed to retain some of the tranquil ambience of old, especially in the West

Bay area north of Seven Mile Beach. This is where visitors can still see examples of traditional architecture, in close proximity to the modern luxury homes in areas such as The Shores. They include wattle-and-daub houses supported by ironwood posts, typical of those erected on Cayman from the 17th to the early-19th centuries, and elaborately decorated cottages built by seamen in the early 20th century. The National Trust offers walking tours of the historical centre of West Bay.

A number of cottage industries still thrive around West Bay, usually run by older ladies. They produce and sell everything from shell jewellery to

crocheted items – all as distinctive as the lilting drawl of West Bayers' speech.

Locals are proud of Barkers Park, on the northeastern flank of the peninsula. Bordered by beaches to the north and low-lying mangrove swamps to the south, it is an important protected habitat for local flora and fauna.

For the sporting-minded, the district has a fine links golf course at Safehaven. The marina at Morgan's Harbour is also a good spot for heading off to nearby Stingray City in North Sound, where visitors and swimmers can get up close and personal with the friendly stingrays. For this adventure alone, it is well worth coming to West Bay.

The Old Homestead

A gift from Hell

Barkers Park

Welcome to Hell!

A picture of Hell

WEST BAY

Public beach

Fisherman at Morgan's Harbour

The Governor's Residence

Riding at Barkers Beach

Sea view from Boggy Sand Road

A local church

Divers close to Boatswains Point

Boatswain's Beach
Home of the world-famous Turtle Farm

Turtles swimming in the lagoon

Boatswain's Beach, situated in West Bay, is Grand Cayman's largest and most prestigious tourist attraction. Pronounced 'Bo-suns' Beach, this one-of-a-kind, 23-acre marine theme park is one of the most exciting in the Caribbean.

Located, some eight miles north of George Town, the US$44 million marine park offers visitors a unique opportunity to swim and snorkel with fish and other marine life in its vast (1.3 million gallon or 4.9 million litre) salt-water lagoon. They can also peer into a predator tank and come nose to nose with sharks and eels.

Slightly less adventurous visitors can wander through the beautiful free-flight bird aviary and listen to the sound of indigenous birds. Or they can stroll down an historic Caymanian street complete with porch-side artisans and craft vendors. The touch pool enables children and adults alike to interact with starfish, urchins and crabs. Should visitors begin to feel hungry, they can enjoy the finest Caymanian cuisine at a variety of locations throughout the park, including a two-storey, full-service restaurant.

The idea for the park was born in November 2001, after Hurricane Michelle caused irreparable damage to the existing Cayman Turtle Farm. Although the Farm was able to resume operations on a more limited basis very quickly, there was little doubt that a complete reconstruction and expansion were required. In the weeks that followed, there were many meetings involving members of the public, government and private sector, planning teams and construction engineers. Together they came up with the plans for Boatswain's Beach.

The breeding pond, opened in December 2002, houses adult Green Sea Turtles. Visitors can view these amazing creatures – which can grow up to 100 lbs (45 kg) – gliding gracefully through the water. The luckiest

A popular destination for tourists

Me and Mr. Turtle

Coming up for air

visitors may even see a female sea turtle going ashore to nest.

Although a world-class attraction, the park faithfully upholds its local heritage. "The park's theme promises to be uniquely Caymanian," explains Ken Hydes, Managing Director of Boatswain's Beach. "The celebration of our culture has remained in the forefront of all planning decisions."

He continues: "Increasingly, it is recognised that today's travelling public are interested in experiencing a country's culture and these are elements that have remained fundamental to the project. It is our objective to ensure the landscapes, marine life, flora and fauna featured in the park are predominantly those indigenous to these Islands."

As part of this emphasis on Cayman's heritage, the historic Cayman Turtle Farm is making its new home within Boatswain's Beach. The only one of its kind in the world, the Turtle Farm is home to over 14,000 Green Sea Turtles. They are the world's largest reptile (by weight),

ranging in size from six ounces (170 grams) for the babies to six hundred pounds (272 kg) each. It takes 15 to 50 years for one of these creatures to reach maturity and some live to the ripe old age of 100.

The Farm hosts more than 500,000 visitors every year and is a fun outing for children and adults, providing an invaluable link between modern Cayman and its seafaring past. The Farm continues to be operational even as Boatswain's Beach grows around it. Visitors can tour a working farm, which is both educational and entertaining, and turtles are available for guests to hold for an amazing and unique photo opportunity.

The Cayman Turtle Farm has a long-standing tradition of releasing some of the turtles bred there. This tradition was initially inspired by its commitment to both of its conservation initiatives: ensuring the continuation of the species and the on-going research that will help biologists learn more about turtle migration and nesting behaviour. Visitors to the island

can actively participate in an annual turtle release, a once-in-a-lifetime experience. Full details are on the Farm's website.

The Turtle Farm breeds the Green Sea Turtle, which takes its name from the green colour of the fat deposits inside its skin. Although feeding is not at exact times, the turtles are fed in the morning and the afternoon. If visitors happen to arrive before feeding time, these graceful creatures are likely to swim right up to them at the pool's edge. There can be few better opportunities to observe sea turtles up close. Other turtle species exhibited here include the Loggerhead, the Kemps Ridley and the beautifully patterned Hawksbill.

Thanks to the newly expanded facilities at Boatswain's Beach, which is open seven days a week, visitors can continue to learn more about these amazing sea creatures. For the new park – which is one of the Caribbean's top tourist attractions – houses a world-class research and educational facility focusing on the conservation of sea turtles.

The turtle is a very agile swimmer

A young hatchling

Boatswain's Beach

A turtle bred at the farm being released offshore

Feeding time

Radiant beauty of the turtle's shell

The exquisite facial marking of an adult sea turtle

A school visit

The lagoon

Turtle Farm resident

Reception centre

The TeleCayman head office situated in the Cayman Corporate Centre, George Town

Telecommunications leader

At the heart of the Cayman Islands' success as an international business centre is an impressive, forward-looking telecommunications infrastructure. Served by a monopoly for many years, the Islands' telecommunications sector saw the exciting process of liberalisation unfold in July 2003, following its initiation the previous year by

the Government. The local telecoms liberalisation is widely regarded as having been smooth and efficient, compared to the process elsewhere in the Caribbean region.

The Islands' telecommunications sector is supported by an equally world-class regulatory framework, in the form of the Information and

Communications Technology Authority (ICTA), an independent statutory authority created by the ICTA Law, (2002). The Cayman Islands' progressive outlook was demonstrated in the telecommunications sector when, as a result of the ICTA Law, they became one of the first countries in the world to officially recognise the convergence of

First-class customer care

Corporate Account Manager with client

132

TeleCayman engineer

The personal touch

The launch of TeleCayman was thus a significant event in the liberalisation roll-out and the company became the incumbent's first competitor in the provision of fixed-line phone services. Mrs Gloria Glidden, President and Chief Operating Officer, vividly recalls the excitement of taking up the challenge presented by full and open competition in this sector. She also expressed her delight that the people of Cayman are now able to enjoy the benefits which flow from competition – including lower prices, a higher level of service quality, and innovation.

"We are proud to be the first alternative provider of fixed lines in the history of the Cayman Islands, and are dedicated to ensuring that our customers receive the exceptional quality of product and service levels that they expect and deserve," said Mrs Glidden at the launch of the company.

Located in the prestigious Cayman Corporate Centre in the heart of George Town, the jurisdiction's business capital, TeleCayman provides local and long-distance voice, private-line circuits, residential and business Internet to the Islands. The company has taken a lead role in making competition a reality in the area of fixed-line phone service in the Islands. It is now taking the telecommunications sector forward in service areas which are critical for many of the world's top international financial institutions and other businesses which operate from the Cayman Islands, as well as for residences in the country.

As underlined in the regulators' recent assessment of the market, the company has clearly had a major and immediate impact on the sector. "The benefits of competition that consumers have seen in the mobile market are now spreading to the fixed market," said David Archbold, Managing Director of the ICTA.

To illustrate the success of the liberalisation effort in the Islands, over 65 new prefixes for phone numbers have been issued by the ICTA to fixed-line and mobile companies. TeleCayman uses the '769' and '825' prefixes.

The firm is the sister company of TeleBermuda International, the dominant telecommunications operator in Bermuda, another leading international business centre. Drawing on its sister company's experience and world-class technical and customer-service standards, TeleCayman offers local businesses and residents high-quality, reliable and cost-effective communications.

While there are currently no official ICTA statistics in the Cayman Islands, it is clear that the data/Internet market is poised for growth. TeleCayman is ideally positioned to participate in this sector's future success.

Local telecommunications suffered a setback in September 2004, after Hurricane Ivan hit Grand Cayman. However, most of the sector's service providers scrambled to restore normal service as quickly as possible and the Islands' telecommunications infrastructure was soon up and running again. TeleCayman played its role in this speedy recovery, deploying teams of engineers who worked around the clock. Today the Islands' telecommunications sector has fully recovered and TeleCayman has been actively rolling out its services to both new business and residential clients in the newly liberalised marketplace.

Companies in the international business and tourism industries have been the backbone of the economic success of the Cayman Islands, the world's fifth-largest financial centre and a first-class tourist destination. These companies require reliable and cost-effective telecommunications, delivered with the highest customer-service standards. By calling on technical standards that rank among the highest in the world as well as an impressive team of technical experts and customer-care representatives, TeleCayman is busy taking the Islands' telecommunications sector into a new era of success.

Highly trained installation technicians

telephony, radio and broadcasting, the Internet and e-business.

Since the start of the liberalisation process, 26 local companies across these various areas have been licensed by the ICTA. At the last count, there were almost 10,000 main lines in the Islands, representing around 24 main lines per 100 persons. During the first year of liberalisation, much of the roll-out activity concentrated on the re-licensing of existing companies in areas such as radio and broadcasting under the new legislation, as well as on the introduction of a few mobile-telephone service providers. Up until then, however, competition was lacking in one key area targeted by the Government's liberalisation's policy – that of fixed-line phone services, which are so vital for many businesses and residences.

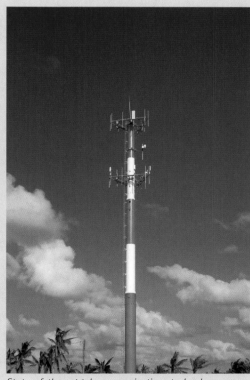
State-of-the-art telecommunications technology

First in mobile communications

The West Indies cricket team, sponsored by Digicel

Digicel is the Cayman Islands' leading mobile service provider and a major contributor to the local economy. Its extensive range of products and services supports an international business community along with a diverse and cosmopolitan population.

Present in fifteen countries in the Caribbean, where it is the fastest-growing mobile telecommunications provider, the company offers 100% coverage in the Cayman Islands. Its GSM network delivers crystal-clear communications, competitive rates and first-class customer service.

Digicel entered the Cayman Islands market in March 2004, within six months of the liberalisation of the telecoms market. By investing over $20 million in its network and offering innovative promotions, products and services, the company has become the No.1 mobile operator within its first year of operation. Many of the new mobile products and services introduced here were a first for the Cayman Islands. These include prepaid roaming (pan-Digicel Caribbean Islands, the UK and other new destinations coming soon) and rollover minutes (giving customers on postpaid plans their unused minutes the following month). Prepaid customers have several options to top-up, including over 100 FLEX card retailers throughout the Islands as well as WebFLEX online top-up service and the FlexEcard service allowing customers to top-up at Butterfield Bank ATM cash machines. The company also claimed a world first with the launch of Digicel WORLD. This postpaid plan offers a flat rate of 20 cents to call mobile or fixed-line numbers anywhere in the world.

International communications links are vital for the Islands, helping to support their thriving financial and tourist industries. Digicel's constant focus on value for money enables customers to cost-effectively stay connected to the outside world. Its international call rates are significantly lower than those of its competitors. Highly competitive local rates are also available to fixed-line and Digicel mobile numbers through the FLEX prepaid and SELECT postpaid plans.

Customers who travel abroad can take advantage of Digicel's comprehensive roaming service, with the ability to use their mobiles in more than 100 countries with over 180 international service providers. As well as voice services, Digicel also provides a comprehensive range of other services. These include text and picture messaging and a wide selection of ringtones, pictures and logos to personalise their phone. Corporate customers can call on an extensive range of tailored services, allowing them to work and communicate anytime and anywhere. The Digicel Corporate packages enable companies to select the services they require with innovative packages tailored to individual companies' needs. Rates are highly competitive and customers can share minutes between users. Digicel also has an innovative product (Digicel Corporate Group) which enables companies to make unlimited calls to one another for a low monthly fee. This service can also include prepaid phones, allowing companies to manage their telecoms costs whilst running their business efficiently.

Besides providing Cayman customers with the most competitive worldwide rates, Digicel offers various state-of-the-art PDA (personal digital assistant) phones. Equivalent to having a mobile office in the hand, these feature-rich devices provide e-mail, calendar, contacts and task information for all business needs. The company also provides a complete telecoms solution with fixed services offering a range of voice, data and Internet products.

Though a relative newcomer to the Islands, Digicel is known for its corporate responsibility programmes. They strengthen Caribbean communities by addressing education, youth, social and cultural needs. Local projects are driven by employees willing to devote their skills and time to helping others. That dedication mirrors a company-wide commitment to roll out the most innovative mobile services throughout the Cayman Islands.

Staying in touch

Mobile phones to suit all tastes

Power to the people

Laying submarine transmission cables to enhance reliability across the island

In the growing community of Grand Cayman, providing world-class service is a top priority at Caribbean Utilities Company, Ltd. ('CUC'), the island's only public electric utility company. CUC commenced its operations on the island in May 1966 under an exclusive licence from the Government. The company, which serves approximately 20,000 customers, is

Employees worked long hours to restore service following Hurricane Ivan

currently in negotiations with the Government to extend the licence beyond its scheduled expiration in January 2011.

Considered one of the most reliable and efficient power companies in the Caribbean, CUC has been through many challenging and exciting periods but has kept pace with Grand Cayman's rapid growth since 1966. This growth has allowed CUC to expand its customer base and to become a leader in the hiring and training of Caymanians, as well as a model of corporate citizenship.

Keeping pace with Grand Cayman's development has challenged this publicly traded

electric utility to become technology-driven and deliver world-class and innovative enhancements in its approach to meeting significant customer growth. The company has been listed on the Toronto Stock Exchange since 1990 in United States funds under the trading symbol CUP.U. It currently has more than 1,300 local shareholders and a market capitalisation of over US$300 million.

Fortis Energy (Bermuda) Ltd., a subsidiary of Fortis Inc. ('Fortis'), is the largest individual shareholder with approximately 37% of the issued and outstanding shares. Fortis is a diversified international electric utility holding company based in St. John's, Newfoundland, Canada, with investments in regulated electric utilities in Canada, Belize, the USA and Grand Cayman. CUC has enjoyed a strong relationship with Fortis for more than a decade and has benefited tremendously from numerous operational and strategic synergies created by the partnership.

When operating an electric utility on a relatively flat island, like tropical Grand Cayman, weather is always a factor that needs to be taken into consideration – especially during hurricane season, which runs from June to November. In September 2004, CUC was greatly affected by Hurricane Ivan, a category-five storm. The restoration of service to all re-connectable customers was completed by the end of November 2004.

The successful restoration programme would

CUC supports environmental education programmes

not have been possible without the commitment of the company's dedicated employees, who currently number just under 200. They were assisted by Fortis and MasTec (USA), the company's strategic partners, as well as CARILEC, the Caribbean's electric utility association that deployed emergency line crews.

CUC is reaping the benefits of strategic alliances for generation and transmission and distribution with MAN B&W Diesel AG (Germany) and ABB Power T&D, Inc. (USA), respectively. It has added approximately 45 MegaWatts of generating capacity through MAN B&W and commissioned four substations across the island through ABB.

These two strategic alliances provide the company with 'most preferred customer' pricing. Other advantages of these agreements include improved design and construction, shorter delivery lead times and standardisation of equipment, parts and training.

Higher exhaust stacks improve air quality on the island

Protection of Grand Cayman's fragile environment is of paramount importance to CUC – which was granted the internationally recognised ISO 14001:1996 environmental standard by the International Organisation for Standardisation in 2004. The company was recertified in June 2005 using the ISO 14001:2004 standard. This certification marks international achievement and recognition of the company's environmental protection and performance in respect of electric power generation. In keeping with its vision to provide world-class energy services, CUC, the first local organisation to receive this certification, has developed an environmental policy to ensure that it operates in an environmentally conscious manner and to conserve natural resources.

Sailing on a luxury catamaran

World-class watersports

Synonymous with luxury watersports since 1988, Red Sail Sports offers a wide range of fun-in-the-sun activities, from diving and snorkelling to sailing. The Cayman-based company is also a leader in watersports equipment, with nineteen retail stores.

Grand Cayman is one of the world's greatest dive destinations, renowned for its warm, crystal-clear water, its stretches of magnificent and unspoiled coral reefs, schools of colourful fish and friendly stingrays. The island is famous too for its spectacular shipwrecks, vertical walls teeming with sea life and dramatic underwater drop-offs.

One of the best ways to explore this underwater beauty is through Red Sail Sports, the only company delivering full-service dive and watersports services island-wide. It maintains seven full-service dive and watersports beach sites, located on Grand Cayman's North, West and East sides, and has a number of retail and booking centres, including at the Hyatt Regency Hotel, Westin Casuarina Hotel, Marriott Beach Resort, Courtyard Marriott Hotel, Morritt's Tortuga Club, Rum Point, and Sea Grape Beach.

Certified scuba divers may enjoy daily one- and two-tank dives at any of the 160 chartered dive sites on Grand Cayman. Night dives are also available and offer a sneak peak at the nocturnal behaviour of the underwater inhabitants. For non-certified divers, the company provides one-day introductory dive courses as well as full certifications and continuing education courses.

Specific programmes are aimed at the budding young diver. Under PADI's innovative Bubblemaker programme, kids aged 8 to 11 can try their underwater skills in the resort pool. Under-8s can experience scuba with the SASY programme (snorkel with scuba), especially designed to let the very young breath on scuba equipment without going under the water.

Fully equipped catamarans are available for exploring the seas around the island. The

Stingray City

136

Relaxing on board

Water-skiing

company owns and runs four state-of-the-art vessels, ranging in size from the 42-foot Far Tortuga to the 65-foot Spirit of Poseidon. They are expertly crewed by staff whose sole purpose is to provide service and customer satisfaction. Built in the United States

picturesque setting, "real" island atmosphere, hammocks on the beach and the Wreck Bar – celebrated for its refreshing tropical drinks, along with delicious barbecue and island fare. The water is very shallow and clear here, perfect for swimming, snorkelling or just lazing around on a raft. A glass-bottom boat takes snorkellers to the Stingray City Sandbar and nearby coral reefs.

Guests are invited to visit one of the retail outlets at any of the hotels serviced by Red Sail Sports. Most of the shops carry a comprehensive selection of T-shirts, casual wear and designer swimwear for all the family, as well as gift and sundry items and holiday necessities such as film, cameras and sunglasses.

Today one of the world's leading resort watersports operators, Red Sail Sports remains dedicated to its original philosophy of helping people have fun and combining the highest standards of service with top-of-the-line equipment. The company continually adds new activities and equipment to its fleet and is proud to have a loyal repeat clientele.

The Atlantis submarine

Exploring the underwater world

Virgin Islands, the catamarans were designed with the comfort of guests in mind. They feature plenty of cabin space, trampoline nets for sunbathing, ample shade and restroom facilities.

Red Sail Sports offers two snorkelling sails to the world-famous Stingray City, one including lunch and the other an afternoon excursion without lunch. Guests are even encouraged to pet and play with the friendly Southern Stingrays. Sunset Sails and Dinner Sails are the perfect way to end a relaxing day in Grand Cayman.

No visit to the island is complete without a trip to the beautiful North Side and the famous Rum Point. The Rum Point Club has long been famous for its

Trip to Stingray Sandbar by glass-bottom boat

Fun above and below

The Cayman Islands have many natural land treasures, but the most spectacular treasures are found below the surface of the water. Grand Cayman, Cayman Brac and Little Cayman are the peaks of mountains, rising steeply from some of the world's deepest ocean waters off the Cayman Trench. The low-lying land masses, surrounded by sheer drop-offs in all directions, allow visitors to experience some of the cleanest ocean water – teeming with colourful tropical marine life, vibrant sponges and extensive, healthy reef formations.

There are many ways for young and old to explore these beautiful waters, which are renowned as one of the world's top scuba diving destinations. Dive operators on all three islands help enthusiasts to experience underwater adventures – made famous by French marine explorer Jacques Cousteau – in a myriad of ways.

Certified divers may dive morning, noon and night. Recreational dive depths are adhered to and the best operators are members of the Cayman Islands Tourism Association (CITA). Divers may explore to a maximum depth of 130 feet (40 metres) any of the famous Cayman 'walls', which are studded with deep canyons, caves and river-like sand chutes disappearing from 60 to 80 feet (18 to 24 m) down into the deep blue depths. These walls are covered with

Parasailing

spectacular sponge and coral growth, including giant orange elephant ear sponges and beautiful black coral trees. Some operators also offer courses in technical diving that allow even greater depths and times underwater.

While the deep walls are undoubtedly alluring and spellbinding, the shallow reefs and wrecks on all islands are equally captivating, abounding with thousands of tropical fish and marine creatures. These sites, ranging in depth from five to 50 feet (1.5 to 15 m), open the underwater world to hundreds of thousands of snorkellers annually.

Those who do not want to get wet may take a trip on a submarine or semi-submersible on Grand Cayman. Submarines take people on adventures in shallow waters or as deep as 800 feet (244 m) on the two-man vessel operated by Atlantis Submarines. The impressive Atlantis XI can accommodate 45 people and dive to 100 feet (30 m), while the Bubble Sub allows fun and

The lure of the deep

A romantic evening cruise

Waverunner off Seven Mile Beach

138

the waves

Diving from Sunset House

Snorkellers' paradise

want to see the rays and stay dry (though people can also get off and snorkel).

Activities on the water rather than under also abound. Visitors can take a thrilling Waverunner ride or they can parasail at altitudes up to 300 feet (90 m) for a bird's-eye view of the reefs and wall. Other popular activities include kayaking, aqua-trike rides, water skiing, sailing or simply floating in the warm sun on a raft and dreaming the day away.

Keen fishermen should try their hand at world-class deep sea fishing for species such as marlin,

excitement for two people with 360-degree vision at depths down to 60 feet (18 m).

Grand Cayman's Stingray City and the Stingray Sandbar are among the world's most famous marine interaction experiences. Visitors can take a trip into the North Sound and play with Southern stingrays in water ranging from three to 12 feet (one to four metres) deep. After seeing these wonderful creatures hand fed by their guide, people soon understand why they are the island's favourite pets. These trips are

Nautilus semi-sub

A traditional Catboat

by motor boat or comfortable and stable sailing catamarans.

Close to the Stingray Sandbar is famous Rum Point, a must-see land stop. The spectacular, child-friendly beach and waters are serviced with an array of water-sport toys and diving, as well as a glass-bottom boat for those who

tuna, mahi-mahi and wahoo. Alternatively, they can test their skills in the shallows with some light tackle for reef fish or the famous Little Cayman bone fish.

And the perfect way to end a day spent in or under the water? By common consent, nothing beats a memorable sunset cocktail cruise or a romantic seated dinner sail by candlelight under the Caribbean stars.

Catamaran crew

Kayak safari

Stingray City & Sandbar

North Wall diving sites and the North Sound Stingray Sandbar

Close encounter with a friendly stingray

Stingray Sandbar, the Cayman's most popular attraction

Stingray City and Sandbar have long been the Cayman Islands' top attractions. Situated in the North Sound, these two sites are favourites with divers and snorkellers, who come to enjoy the crystal-clear blue sea and colourful marine life. Yet the main attraction will always be the stingrays. Arriving by boat, visitors are encouraged to swim in the 12-foot (4-metre) deep waters at Stingray City and allow these graceful creatures to glide amongst them. The shallow waters at the Sandbar allow people to stand up and gently pet the friendly rays or feed them with portions of succulent squid. A close encounter of the strangest kind!

Feeding a stingray at Stingray City

Stingray Sandbar

Snorkelling with the stingrays

Stingray City

Agriculture

Bananas are widely cultivated

Seasoning pepper seedlings

Mangoes ripening in the Cayman sunshine

Willie Ebanks' pig farm, the island's largest

Locally reared livestock

June Plums

A family tradition

From humble beginnings over 35 years ago, the Hurley Merren family has developed its food-supply business into one of the Cayman Islands' most respected companies.

This family-owned business started as an idea of Mr Gail Hurley Merren, while he worked in the airline industry. He decided to import produce, fresh meats, seafood and dairy products from Costa Rica for consumers in the Cayman Islands. The business developed quickly and by 1973 Cayman Imports Ltd had built its first warehouse on Walkers Road in George Town. A great deal of development has since taken place in this area, but this was one of the first commercial building there.

The business continued to prosper and in 1982 the first Hurley's Meat Market opened. It operated until the opening of Hurley's Supermarket in the Eden Centre in 1986.

Cayman Imports has seen massive expansion over the years. A 24,000 square-foot warehouse was built in 1991 and the company's administrative offices moved to the old Hurley's Meat Market Building. Today Cayman Imports is a major food service distributor supplying restaurants, grocers and other businesses with a number of leading products.

Since the first store's opening in the Eden Centre, Hurley's Supermarket has been a successful and resilient business. It expanded rapidly in the late 1990s, with the opening of a smaller Lil' Hurley's in East End in 1998 and the flagship store at the Grand Harbour Centre, Red Bay in 1999.

Hurricane Ivan, which left a trail of devastation when it passed by Grand Cayman in September 2004, completely destroyed two of the Hurley's properties, The Eden Centre and Lil' Hurley's. However, the Merren family is committed to rebuilding both supermarkets even bigger and better than before to serve the communities.

The Grand Harbour store weathered the storm well with limited damage and the Merren family, as well as their dedicated employees, worked hard in the storm's immediate aftermath to re-open it. As a result, Hurley's Marketplace at Grand Harbour was the first supermarket to open post-Ivan and became a lifeline for Cayman Islands' residents needing essential supplies.

Sadly, the Hurley's group founder passed away in June 1997. His wife, Mrs Leonie Merren-Ebanks, and her four children have retained management of the businesses and even diversified into other areas. The Merrens' eldest son Bryce manages Cayman Imports, while younger son Randy assists with the running of the supermarket as well as the family's latest venture, Hurley's Entertainment Corporation. The company also employs both of the Merrens' daughters. Shanna is the Human Resource Manager and Sharleen assists Bryce with the managing of Cayman Imports.

Hurley's Entertainment Corporation has diversified the range of products offered by the family. The company runs two popular local radio stations: Z99, the Islands' first privately owned radio station, and Rooster 101, the only local country and western music station.

There are plans to expand further into the communications and entertainment market. Recently, the Information and Communications Technology Authority (ICTA) granted a licence to Hurley's Entertainment Corporation to offer digital cable television, high-speed broadband Internet service and Voice over Internet Protocol (VoIP) digital telephony via a fibre optic network. In terms of quality, reliability, performance and speed, fibre optic technology – which transmits huge amounts of information at light speed – will offer Grand Cayman telecommunications benefits far superior to anything currently available.

The taste of the Caribbean

The romantic Pappagallo restaurant in West Bay

Bacchus, for fine wines and good food

Cayman's earliest settlers survived on what many doctors might now prescribe as one of the world's healthiest diets. Turtle, fish, conch, whelk and 'breadkind' – meaning high fibre starch crops such as cassava, yam and sweet potato – formed the average Caymanian's basic diet until fairly recently. Beef was a prized delicacy, usually reserved for festivals such as Christmas. This diet was supplemented by fruit such as plantain, banana, mango, ginep, guava or papaya, depending on the season. It may sound bland by modern standards, but was unusually healthy and many Caymanians of earlier generations lived very long lives. Before the advent of fast-food outlets, centenarians were not uncommon in Cayman. More recently, immigrant labourers from Jamaica, Cuba and Honduras have brought with them their own native dishes, spicing up this traditional fare.

Many local restaurants cater to the tastes of this group of Caribbean peoples – most tend to eat at lunchtime, and any visitor wishing to try genuine local or regional food should lunch at Champion House, Singh's Roti Shop (Trinidad), Luz's (Honduras) or Welly's Cool Spot (Jamaica) for example. Menus feature conch stew, jerk chicken (seasoned, marinated and slow smoked over a low fire), Jamaican ackee (the national fruit of Jamaica) and codfish, snapper 'Cayman style', and pork, beef and chicken cooked in any number of ways – well spiced and tasty. Rarely served plain, rice is usually served with beans or peas (Jamaica) or with black beans (Cuba).

In recent times the Islands have enjoyed phenomenal growth driven by tourism and offshore finance, accompanied by an influx of professionals, including chefs, from all over the world. Cayman has developed a selection of restaurants which are the envy of the Caribbean. Their owners and staff hail from the United States, Europe and as far afield as Asia. As a result, locals and visitors alike can enjoy first-class food and fine dining at establishments dotted around the Islands, though the vast majority are located in Grand Cayman.

Competitive pressure and a relatively affluent and demanding clientele have pushed the standard of cuisine in Cayman's restaurants to a new level. Well-known names include Bacchus, Edoardo's, Ragazzi, Pappagallo, Calypso Grill, Grand Old House, The Brasserie and Hemingway's.

Most of these restaurants base their dishes on local seafood – wahoo, tuna, mahi-mahi, and red snapper can usually be relied upon to be fresh. Shrimp and lobster (really langoustine or Caribbean spiny lobster) are usually imported frozen. The taking of local lobster and conch is restricted to a short season by Cayman's Marine Protection Laws. Turtle is completely protected but farmed turtle from the West Bay Turtle Farm occasionally finds itself on a menu – most often as turtle stew in a local restaurant.

Until 30 years ago only beer, spirits and a very rudimentary selection of wines could be found. Now wine is imported from virtually every

Al fresco dining at the Calypso Grill

major wine-producing nation on Earth. Pre-eminent among Cayman wine retailers is the Jacques Scott Fine Wine Store, with a selection of over 800 wines.

Hemingway's, a local favourite

The friendly atmosphere of Edoardo's

A diversified distributor

The Jacques Scott Group is the Cayman Islands' leading wholesaler and retailer of wine, beer and spirits as well as a distributor of a wide range of soft drinks, food and food-related services to the hotel, restaurant and retail sectors.

From modest origins more than a half century ago, Jacques Scott has become a major Cayman company. Its four operating divisions employ some 100 people, many of whom are proud shareholders in the business. Its current Managing Director, Peter Dutton, joined the company more than two decades ago after honing his skills as an accountant.

The company started out as a beer and spirits importer, with a limited range of food products, wines and champagnes. Today it is one of the Islands' leading food distributors and supplies food to all local supermarkets. In Florida, it controls three companies which act as wholesalers of fresh produce, and as buyers and sellers of restaurant equipment and food for the Cayman Islands and the Caribbean generally.

Working through its Alcoholic Beverage Division, the firm is the Islands' largest distributor of wine, beer and spirits. The finest French, Italian and American wines, among

them Antinori, Gaja, Bertani, Moet & Chandon, Jadot, Drouhin, Jolivet, Jaboulet, Ridge, Shafer and Beringer to name just a few, make up the bulk of the company's wine-import business. It also imports wines from Australia, New Zealand, Spain, Portugal, Chile, Germany and South Africa, and draws up wine lists for some of the top local restaurants.

Jacques Scott is exclusive distributor for Heineken, Cayman's best-selling beer. Its beer distribution also takes in Coors Light, made in the United States, Amstel Light and a range of beers from Canadian brewer Labatt. It is also an exclusive distributor for the world's largest drinks company Diageo, maker of spirits such as Smirnoff Vodka, Johnnie Walker, Crown Royal Canadian whisky and Baileys Irish Cream, to mention but a few. It also represents Appleton Rum, the most popular rum in the Cayman Islands.

The Food Division wholesales branded goods from manufacturers worldwide, spanning everything from breakfast cereals to mineral waters. The company is an exclusive distributor for Nestlé, the world's leading food group, and Kraft Foods. It stocks a comprehensive range of their products, including Carnation milk, Nescafé coffee, Maggi soups, Planters peanuts and Nabisco snacks and bakery products.

The third of the four divisions, Island Supply

Company Limited, provides food, catering and food-service supplies to hotels, restaurants and institutions in Cayman, the Caribbean and Central America. It designs and installs complete kitchens and bar equipment for clients and has an attractive showroom that is open to both the trade and general public, displaying commercial equipment for home use.

Under the Retail Division, the company operates seven stores throughout Grand Cayman. Four are duty-paid wine and spirits outlets in the George Town/Seven Mile Beach areas, including the renowned Jacques Scott Fine Wine Store. It also runs the biggest duty-free store in the departure lounge of Grand Cayman's Owen Roberts International Airport, as well as a gift store in the check-in area. On the George Town waterfront, the company has a franchise for La Casa Del Habano, purveyor of prestige Cuban cigars. Lastly, it has a share in two duty-free liquor stores in George Town, Dick's Liquor and Pirates' Grotto.

Known locally for its strong commitment to the community and support for many different charities, Jacques Scott remains equally dedicated to growing its business in Cayman and beyond.

Everyone has their favourite table

First for food, service and style

A favourite with knowledgeable residents and tourists alike, The Brasserie serves eclectic, modern cuisine. The restaurant in the heart of George Town's financial district is also renowned for its decor, which successfully blends styles as varied as traditional British with Caribbean colonial.

With Brasserie catering, perfect for meetings and training

Affectionately dubbed 'The Brass' by locals, the establishment has been owned and run by Lisa and Clarence Flowers since it opened in 1997. Its elegant yet informal decor – featuring authentic Mexican terracotta tiles, furniture from England and Indonesia, Jamaican masks and a traditional Cayman tongue and groove ceiling – owes much to the time and effort invested by the couple in achieving the right environment and atmosphere for guests.

The restaurant is famed for its sophisticated and diverse cuisine, prepared from first-class ingredients delivered daily to the kitchen. A typical menu includes a selection of fresh soups, salads, pasta, meat and seafood dishes, rounded off with a variety of delicious desserts. Additional menus are available for lunch and dinner, either à la carte or pre-set with two or three courses to accommodate groups and parties. All are served with a variety of breads baked in-house.

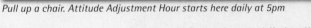

Pull up a chair. Attitude Adjustment Hour starts here daily at 5pm

Menus are adapted every day, according to the chefs' whims and creativity, among them special set menus for holidays and Sundays. Guests arriving on a Wednesday evening may also sample the blind tasting menu, 'Blind Sided', which gives pride of place to a series of small dishes inspired by the cuisine of the Caribbean, Asia, India and France. Each of these dishes is paired with a carefully selected wine. Every weekday, from 5pm to 10pm, the establishment also serves a platter of tapas to groups of two or more guests, accompanied by their favourite wine or cocktails.

The Brasserie staff are always on hand to assist diners with any questions they may have about the food menu or wine list. Available by the glass or bottle, the wine includes an extensive selection of the finest white and red vintages from the world's leading wine-producing countries. The restaurant also serves superior champagnes, such as Dom Perignon and Veuve Clicquot.

The owners have extended their facilities over the years, adding a Patio Room which can be reserved for private functions. They also offer a complete cocktail party catering service for functions at home, in the office or elsewhere. First-class conference facilities – located close to the restaurant in the Century Yard building at Cricket Square – are the very latest addition. Geared to the local business community, the state-of-the-art Brasserie Conference Facility caters for up to 70 people in a classic layout or up to 100 in a theatre-style chair configuration, which is ideal for film screenings or other presentations.

This elegantly decorated room, very much in keeping with the contemporary Caribbean style of the neighbouring restaurant, is fitted with a range of high-tech audiovisual and computer equipment. Clients benefit from personalised service as well as a range of catering options provided by the restaurant, ranging from simple snack packages to complete meals.

Whether dining in style or doing business in Cayman's premier meeting venue, every guest of The Brasserie is assured of a memorable experience.

The best in fine dining

The restaurant offers several attractive private dining areas able to accommodate from eight to 280 guests. The outside facilities include a traditional screened-in porch, a seaside verandah right on the water's edge, and charming gazebos (including a spectacular wedding gazebo).

The Main Dining Room is the warm and elegant heart of the establishment. It offers air-conditioned comfort with its adjoining English Room, perfect for private dinners and business meetings for up to 20 guests.

The Wine Room seats a maximum of 10 guests and can be reserved for private wine tastings and intimate dinners or business meetings. This hidden treasure notably features a private entrance and fine wooden wine racks where the finest wines on the island are kept and aged. Grand Old House, it should be noted, has received 19 consecutive awards of excellence from the prestigious Wine Spectator Magazine.

The establishment offers first-class fully licensed island-wide catering services with a full-time wedding coordinator on the staff. Those who enjoy the finest seafood, meat and poultry dishes with the flavour of the Caribbean will be delighted with the chef's extensive offerings.

A legend of Grand Cayman, this former plantation house has marked more than 95 years of elegant history. The grand dame of restaurants remains one of the island's finest with Chef Mathai, who has cooked for presidents and royalty, overseeing guests' culinary experience. Grand Old House has been renowned as Grand Cayman's top restaurant for the last 30 years. It is located in the beautiful surroundings of the South Sound area, just south of the business and retail centre of George Town. The restaurant, on the water's edge, offers its guests unmatched vistas of the crystal-clear Caribbean Sea.

Over the years Grand Old House has attracted visitors from around the world who come to enjoy a variety of international dishes, prepared with a Caribbean flair. Built in 1908, the establishment sets the standard for hosting the island's most refined balls, receptions, parties and other social events. The structure was built originally as part of an old coconut plantation when

William Henry Law, a businessman from Boston, constructed the house out of locally grown ironwood. With its posts fixed directly into Cayman's ironshore, the house has withstood the strongest storms that sometimes occur in the Caribbean.

When Mr. Law left the island, the Lambert family was sent over to live in and look after the stately home. The Lamberts entertained frequently, hosting elegant parties at the house – a tradition it was destined to continue. In later years, Grand Old House served variously as a family home, a Sunday school, a hospital for soldiers wounded in World War II, a shelter for island residents during severe weather and even a beauty parlour.

Thanks to careful preservation and restoration over the intervening decades, the house retains all of its original charm and atmosphere since it was transformed into a restaurant in 1969. At that time, South Sound Road was little more than a dirt track, and the restaurant was lit by oil lamps. Island visitors in those days were few. Nevertheless, Grand Old House became a favourite with local residents and visitors alike.

Today the establishment continues its legend as the venue of choice for fine dining and great atmosphere. It is frequently the site of lavish weddings, exciting birthday parties and memorable business events.

Grand Old House is the perfect blend of romance, cuisine and hospitality. Guests may lunch week days and enjoy dinner nightly, sitting inside or outside with a view of the Caribbean Sea to the accompaniment of live music performed by the world-renowned pianist Vilma Comas.

Grand Old House is where sunset, stars and sea are served . . .

District of Bodden Town

Beach Bay

Historic reflections

The first capital of the Cayman Islands, Bodden Town is today Grand Cayman's largest and fastest-growing district. It stretches from the western suburbs of Savannah as far East as Frank Sound Road, and is some five and a half miles (8.9 km) wide at its widest point.

The area known as South Side by the early settlers was renamed Bodden Town in 1773, when a British map-maker renamed it in honour of the 21 families living there of that name. It was originally a coastal development, as were all early settlements in these Islands. It has developed a blend of modern residential suburbs, while maintaining character with a predominance of 'gingerbread' architecture.

The district claims long-standing local fame, having hosted Cayman's first legislative meeting in 1831. This laid the cornerstone for the

Islands' democratic foundation – at the historically restored three-storey manor house called Pedro St. James 'Castle.' Built in 1780 as a family plantation home, it is now a key tourist attraction and has a multimedia centre that tells the story of the site and of the Cayman Islands in general.

This is the only district to be named after a local family, reflecting the influence of the 'clan' over the years. The original name is not known for certain, but it may have been Bawden, Boden or Boaden, before early settlers changed it to what is today one of the Island's most common surnames. The Boddens have been influential since the 1800s, when there was a 'Governor' and Chief Magistrate by the name of William Bodden. He was instrumental in the construction of the island's

first roads and in development of their early laws.

In 1994, the late James Manoah Bodden – who was elected as a political representative between 1976 and 1984 – was named Cayman's first 'National Hero'. As the Government minister responsible for tourism and aviation, he made great contributions to both. The introduction of the popular 'Pirates Week' festival, held every October to celebrate Cayman's swashbuckling heritage, is attributed to his efforts.

A number of Grand Cayman's best-known sights and monuments are to be found in this district. Located on the western approach to the town, the Guard House served as a defensive outpost for local militiamen on the lookout for pirates or Spanish marauders

Ministry of Agriculture building

Adventist Church

Two 18th-century upturned cannons

Garden furniture-maker Chester Watler

arriving by sea. Little now remains of the original small stone building, first mentioned in a document produced in the 1830s. Nearby Slave Wall, sometimes referred to as Drummond's Wall, was likely built before the emancipation of Cayman slaves and also formed part of the local defences.

Other noteworthy historic sites include the Pirate Cave in the centre of Bodden Town, said to have been used to hide treasure, and the Queen Victoria Monument, a popular meeting spot for locals.

In the early 1900s, the 38-hectare Meagre Bay Pond, just east of Bodden Town, attracted hunters seeking to bag one of the many species of duck found here. The resident and migratory birds eventually deserted the area and have only recently returned in large numbers. The pond is now a Government-designated Animal Sanctuary, adding yet another prime bird-watching site to the many others found on the island.

Monument to the people of Bodden Town

Old Savannah Schoolhouse

149

Bodden Bay

Central Mangrove Wetlands Reserve

District of Bodden Town

The historic Guard House at the entrance to Bodden Town

Pirates Cave

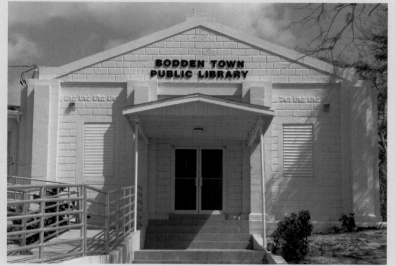
Bodden Town Public Library

The Mangrove Reserve is only accessible by boat

Caymanian cottage, adjacent to the Pirates Cave

Majestic palm trees

Pedro St. James

Birthplace of Caymanian democracy

Grand Cayman's oldest building and its most important historic site is located in Savannah, on the island's south coast. Pedro St. James, also known as Pedro Castle, is an imposing three-storey plantation house standing in landscaped grounds.

Restored to its former glory in the 1990s following a major restoration project, the magnificent solid-stone building offers a historically accurate portrait of an early 19th-century Caribbean plantation house. It was erected on the ruins of a house constructed in 1780 by William Eden, an early Cayman settler and plantation owner. Records show that Eden's original structure was the only one on Grand Cayman to survive the violent hurricane of 1785.

Between 1823 and 1839, the house served as a courthouse and jail. Yet arguably its greatest moment came in December 1831, when it hosted a meeting of Caymanians that led to the establishment of the first elected legislature. As a result, it is today dubbed the 'birthplace of democracy in the Cayman Islands'.

Four years later, history was made again when a proclamation was read out from the building's Palladian staircase announcing the emancipation of local slaves. It is worth

noting that the house's owner, William Eden II, kept more than 20 slaves at the time.

Abandoned in 1877, the house was practically reduced to a stone ruin over the next few decades after being scavenged for building materials. It was bought by Thomas Hubbell in 1954, whose renovations aimed to make it look more like a 'castle'. Sharp-eyed visitors today will notice the date 1631 engraved over an arch, part of Hubbell's efforts to create the illusion that his house was much older than it really is.

In the late 1960s, the building was leased from its owner and turned into a restaurant and hotel. However, it was twice damaged by fire over the next few decades. In 1991, a programme of serious renovation began after the Government purchased the property and its grounds.

Seven years later, Pedro St. James was born again. The restored main house, outer buildings such as the Watler House, Steadman-Bodden House and bake oven, as well as surrounding yards and a garden that includes a woodland trail were opened to the public in January 1998. Later that year, the site saw the opening of a gift shop, restaurant and multimedia Visitors Centre offering a fascinating insight into the history of Pedro St. James and the Cayman Islands in general.

District of North Side

Kaibo Yacht Club

A style of its own

North Side is the island's least populated district and was the last to receive electricity and telecommunications. Its northern shore is best known for its tranquil residential areas. Attracted by idyllic beach-fronts, many North American and European families have built their winter homes in the district over the last four decades. There is, for example, a significant number of luxury waterfront homes around beautiful Cayman Kai.

The northern coastline is mainly rocky and uneven, though around North Sound it comprises mangrove swamps and often takes on the appearance of a muddy river in the rainy season. A number of unique craft stores can be found on the coast, which is a favourite destination with weekend beach-goers and Easter campers.

Rum Point, situated at the tip of the district's peninsula, is a very popular spot with locals and visitors. This lively resort features a broad sandy beach, restaurants, bars, gift shop and a plethora of watersports opportunities. Rum Point can be reached by road or the ferry that crosses North Sound.

Close to Rum Point is the Kaibo Yacht Club, the starting point for the Cayman Islands' Million Dollar Run, a prestigious powerboat race. Complete with marina, restaurant and beach bar, this peaceful little area occasionally hosts major outdoor events. It is also ideal for laid-back sun-seekers or those willing to indulge in a variety of sports in and on the water.

Boating beauties

Kaibo Beach

Race time

Beach Bar

Though the Queen Elizabeth II Botanic Park is situated in East End, its entrance is in North Side, on the Frank Sound Road. A mile or so to the west of this park is the 500-acre (two sq. km) Mastic Reserve and Trail, the latter starting just off Mastic Road. Dating back to the 18th century, the trail was originally intended as a cross-island route for people living in this rather isolated region. It fell into disuse on several occasions and it was not until 1995 that it could be used again, following intensive restoration work by local volunteers.

Today this path meanders through a variety of habitats, including dense virgin woodland and Black Mangrove wetland. Keen-eyed walkers will spot a number of rare species, among them the Wild Banana Orchid and magnificent Mastic tree. They may also glimpse a diverse range of local and migratory birds in the tree canopy – including Cayman's native parrot and the shy Caribbean Dove. The best way to appreciate the trail is to take a guided tour organised by the National Trust, lasting two to three hours.

Malportas Pond is one of the most important brackish ponds on Grand Cayman and an important bird sanctuary. Several hundred West Indian Whistling Ducks can often be seen here, as well as Blue-winged Teal and other waterbirds.

The endangered ducks owe a great deal to the well-known local character and farmer Willie 'Penny' Ebanks. He set aside some of his land adjoining the pond as a sanctuary for the birds and welcomes ornithologist visitors eager to view his 'charges'. Willie's artist brother 'Caribbean Charlie'

and his wife run a nearby shop. Their mainly wooden wares include brightly painted bird-houses fashioned after traditional Cayman cottages and the board-game 'waurie', said to have been played by Blackbeard. But quite what this notorious old pirate would have made of this peaceful little district today is hard to fathom.

– *Kaibo* –

Million Dollar Run, powerboat race

Fun in the sun

Rum Point

Young snorkellers

North Side
— Rum Point —

A popular place to be

Keeping cool

Which way to Brussels?

Beach volleyball

Magnificent Rum Point residence

Siesta time

Relaxing with friends

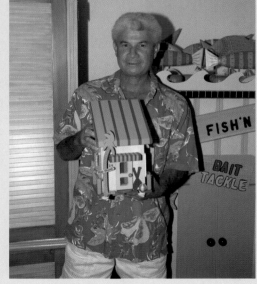
Artist 'Caribbean Charlie' Ebanks

Rum Point jetty

Willie 'Penny' Ebanks, who saved the Whistling Duck from near extinction

Traditional grocery shop

District of North Side

Cracking a conch shell

An unusual pet

Local gift and souvenir shop

Old Man Bay

The Mastic Trail

The magic
of the underwater world

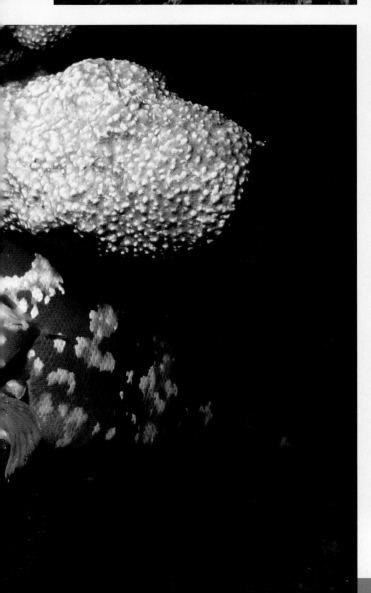

Frank Sound

Colliers Bay

Brass propeller of the freighter Rimandi Mibaju, which sank in 1964 north of Eastward Channel

In harmony with nature

Occupying the eastern tip of Grand Cayman, East End is one of the largest districts. The town of East End is the island's oldest, with origins stretching back to the late 17th century, and once served as an official port of entry. The main road on the northern shore is the Queen's Highway, officially opened by H.M. Queen Elizabeth II as recently as 1983.

Traditional culture and practices, as well as an accompanying spirit of resilience and resourcefulness, are particularly evident here. East Enders, for example, still produce savoury 'potcakes'

made of corn, yam, sweet potatoes and other vegetables, as well as seafood dishes and other culinary delights in the style of their forefathers. Several seaside restaurants and fish-stands in the area are notable for their popularity with residents and visitors alike.

Though locals manage to maintain a laid-back approach to life, the district is also coming into its own in the tourism sector, mainly thanks to the development of beach-side time-share properties. Popular tourist sights include the spectacular blow holes or saltwater geysers in the rough

iron-shore of White Sand Bay. The jets of water gushing out through cracks in the rocks, a product of the pounding waves, never fail to delight visitors.

A little further north along the coast lies Gun Bay, scene of the most famous of the old shipwrecks in this area. The Wreck of the Ten Sails Park commemorates the spot where ships from a large convoy of 58 British merchant vessels came to grief on the treacherous coral reefs during a storm in February 1794.

Ten ships sank, including HMS Convert, the Navy

District of East End

ship leading the convoy. But only eight lives were lost, thanks to the brave rescue efforts of local fishermen. A plaque today relates the historical episode and artefacts of the wrecks can be seen in the National Museum in George Town. For years people speculated that a prince – perhaps the future George IV – had been aboard the leading ship and that a grateful King George III had granted the Islands 'freedom from taxation in perpetuity'. But modern archival research has shown that there is no basis for this colourful old legend.

The eight remaining wrecks are today are among the most popular of Grand Cayman's diving spots. Some of the skeletons of more recent shipwrecks can be spotted from the nearby lighthouse at Gorling Bluff. Built in 1937, this is the third incarnation of the important beacon, now running on solar power. A pretty little park is being created at the site by the National Trust for the Cayman Islands. It features pathways and flower beds that include various medicinal plants once so familiar to islanders.

The Trust was also responsible for establishing the Salina Reserve, an inland area in the north of the district. It covers some 625 acres (2.5 square km) and is made up of a complex mosaic of sedge, buttonwood swamps, dry shrubland and forest. There is no public access, so the reserve remains isolated and undisturbed. This suits the diverse animal and plant life here, including three different types of bat, rare hardwood trees and the captive-bred Blue Iguanas first released in the area in 1993.

East End Post Office

East End is the location of the Queen Elizabeth II Botanic Park, even though its entrance on Frank Sound Road is actually in the district of North Side. Open to the public from 1991, it was officially opened by Her Majesty three years later and has grown in size and scope since. The fascinating 65-acre (0.26 sq. km) park has a vast collection of fauna and flora, the focus being on native species. Visitors can see up to 40% of Grand Cayman's native flora by walking the woodland trail, which passes through a wide variety of habitats. They can also learn about the park's efforts to breed and reintroduce the rare Blue Iguana. The site also has a visitors' centre, several gardens and a lake on which one can see the rare West Indian Whistling Duck.

Another important protected site is found at Colliers Pond, a haven for birdwatchers. Just north of here is The Reef Resort, commonly frequented by watersports enthusiasts. Both peaceful and remote, this beach-side location could be said to characterise the charming East End district in general.

Silver Thatch Palm, the national tree

East End Lighthouse Park at Gorling Bluff

Peaceful country lane

Monument dedicated to the Wreck of the Ten Sails

Queen Elizabeth II Botanic Park
Sixty Five Acres Of Tranquil Beauty

A home from yesteryear

In harmony with nature

Cayman Swallowtail

The protected Blue Iguana, an endangered species endemic to the Cayman Islands

The Banana Orchid, the Islands' national flower

Part of the Floral Colour Garden

A floral masterpiece

A colourful orchid

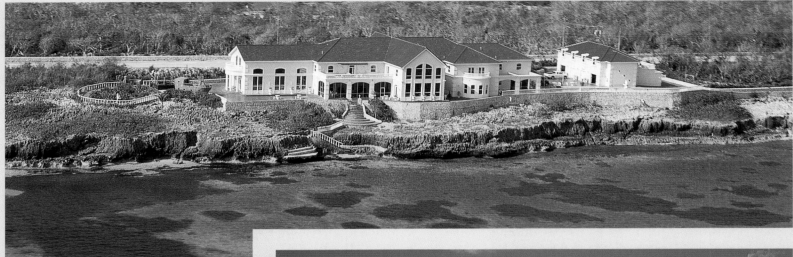

An imposing beach-front mansion

Queen's Highway

Park entrance

District of East End

Another day in paradise

The dramatic blowholes

Rural East End

Relaxing in style

The Reef Resort is an intimate boutique resort located on the quieter side of Grand Cayman in an exquisite East End setting. Situated on the island's largest beach-front resort property, with suites in a selection of two and three-storey buildings set on 1,600 feet (488 m) of pristine white sand on Colliers Bay, it guarantees 'pure beach relaxation' to the discerning traveller.

Unique to Cayman, all of the resort's accommodation is made up of beach-front luxury suites. They come with shady patios and balconies that offer guests cooling sea breezes and magnificent views of the many shades of crystal-clear blue Caribbean waters protected by the reef of Colliers Bay.

Although The Reef is a luxury beach retreat focused on its beach and luxury beach-front suites, it is also a full-service resort allowing guests to plan exactly the type of visit that suits them. Concierge and event-planning staff are available prior to and during guests' visits, to ensure they are able to make the most of the many options available. These include on-site watersports, swimming pools, beach and water volleyball, tennis and a gym.

If guests find that the beach is getting too hot for them, they can cool off at Castro's Hideaway beach bar – home to Castro, the resident Cockatoo, who has many a 'tall' tale to tell. They may also dine in air-conditioned comfort in the restaurant overlooking the ocean, where the concierge is happy to reserve a seat for 'Barefoot night', featuring dinner and dancing and the Barefoot Man – The Reef's resident shoeless Calypsonian and a Cayman institution.

The Reef and its activities are centred around the water. If guests' interests lie above the water, they can go deep-sea fishing or 'explore, discover, preserve' – both on water or on land in the local area – through the in-house tour company, EcoVentures. A further option is simply to enjoy the world-class snorkelling close to the beach.

For activities below the water, The Reef is exclusively partnered with Grand Cayman's premier diving

and snorkelling company, Ocean Frontiers. This company offers 'valet diving' and a level of service and innovation unsurpassed in the dive industry.

The Reef is also an ideal location for hosting events, such as destination weddings, corporate retreats and incentive travel groups. Dedicated event planners at the resort and meeting facilities allow personalised event service, ranging from the smallest groups up to those of 100 or more.

The Reef is also the first beach-front 'condo-hotel' in Cayman. All its suites and condominiums are individually owned, with management provided by the resort. Interested investors may contact any CIREBA (Cayman Islands Real Estate Brokers Association) real estate professional or the listing agents, Century 21.

A bird-watcher's paradise

Western Spindalis

The grand Caymanian Parrot, the national bird

Bananaquit

Caribbean Dove

Red-footed Booby

Loggerhead Kingbird

West Indian Woodpecker

Snowy Egret

Northern Flicker

Vitteline Warbler

Caribbean Whistling Duck

Yucatan Vireo

Little Blue Heron

Greater Antillean Grackle

Dance Cayman Group

Dance Vibes in action

The Rundown satirical revue

Art & Culture

Pirates Week

Story-teller Amina Blackwood-Meeks

Batabano Carnival

Local favourites High-Tide

Camping on the beach at Easter is a popular local custom

Drummer 'Aunt' Julie Hydes

Cayman Drummers

Local legend and calypso singer 'The Barefoot Man'

173

Artist Wray Banker

'Jesus Is Coming', by 'Miss Lassie'

Review's Ciaran Oliver and artist Luelan 'Luts' Bodden

Cayman Islands iconic artist Gladwyn 'Miss Lassie' Bush

Artist 'Caribbean Charlie' Ebanks

Art & Culture

'Peace Be Still', by 'Miss Lassie'

Artist Chris Mann

Weddings Cayman style

As the deep-orange sun slides slowly into the Caribbean, a happy young couple exchange their wedding vows. Surrounded by their nearest and dearest on a gorgeous sandy beach somewhere in Cayman, they are just one of the many couples who journey to this destination every year for the express purpose of getting married.

The Cayman Islands are a magnet for people seeking that extra special wedding, whether indoors or out. They offer spectacular scenery as an unforgettable backdrop, a choice of romantic locations (even beneath the waves for would-be scuba spouses) and are home to some of the world's most experienced wedding organisers. The ceremony and celebrations can be as simple or as sophisticated as the couple want – from an intimate gathering with a few close friends and family to a bumper banquet with entertainment and all the trimmings. And should all go well for the perfect pair, they may well consider returning to the Islands for that extra special anniversary.

175

Cayman Brac

View from the Bluff

An independent spirit

Rebecca's grave inside Rebecca's Cave at South Side, a young victim of the 1932 Hurricane

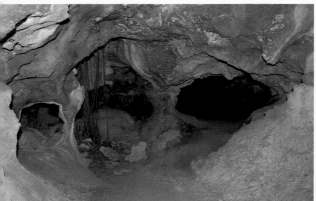

Interior of Bat Cave

The most north-easterly of the three islands, Cayman Brac is located some 90 miles (145 kilometres) from Grand Cayman. Just 12 miles (19.3 km) long and one mile (1.6 km) wide, it is nonetheless blessed with many natural treasures and a rich heritage.

The island derives its name from its most distinctive feature, the Bluff, a limestone cliff rising from sea level in the west to a height of 140 feet (43 m) on the east end. The word 'brac' is Gaelic for 'bluff,' denoting the strong Scottish and Irish ancestry of many Brackers, as the islanders are locally known. 'The Brac' is a mere 30-minute flight away from the contemporary hubbub of Grand Cayman. But many visitors say that the island's fiercely independent, proud and honest people transport them back to a time when life was far simpler and trusting in one's neighbour was taken for granted.

The island supports a close-knit community of fewer than 2,000. These traditionally seafaring people – who once depended on turtling, merchant shipping, thatch-rope production and beachcombing for their livelihood – are largely geared towards tourism today. Yet Cayman Brac is the home of many retired seafarers and is still very much a mariners' community, retaining the essence of its distinctively self-sufficient culture. Many locals still rear a few cattle, chickens and goats for local consumption or to be sold locally. As 'backyard gardeners', they also grow cassava, yams, papaya and mangoes.

The Brac is a birdwatcher's paradise. Starting in Spot Bay, one of the oldest districts in the north-east of the island, a road leads to a winding path that goes up to the side of the Bluff to Peter's Cave and on up to the Bluff itself.

The Honeymoon Cottage!

A traditional island house

A survivor of the 1932 hurricane

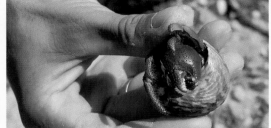

Hermit Crab, known locally as the Soldier Crab

Tanning vats at the Heritage House

Halfway Ground Cave, also known as Skull Cave

The public beach at South Side

The Bluff viewed from the South Side

Brown Booby

This area features Magnificent Frigate Birds and Brown Boobies gliding on air currents that rise from the sheer rock.

Almost 200 migratory bird species can be seen on the island. They include the endangered Cayman Brac parrot, especially on the north coast and on the Bluff's protected woodland reserve. Wetland ponds across the island are also a haven for a wide selection of herons and shorebirds. Among them are the rare West Indian Whistling Duck, for which both Brac and Little Cayman are stopovers on the bird's migratory journey between North and South America.

Cayman Brac has five fascinating caves to explore: the Great Cave, Halfway Ground, Rebecca's, Peter's, and Bat Cave. Other smaller ones also riddle the limestone bluff and local rumour has it that the infamous pirate Edward Teach, or Blackbeard, buried treasure in one of them. It is supposedly still up for the taking! Also called 'hurricane caves,' these rock fissures have served as a refuge from the several violent storms that have pummelled the island over the last two centuries. On the north-eastern side of the Bluff, Peter's Cave is one of the largest and can shelter up to 100 people.

Small as the island is, Cayman Brac has an international airport and a large commercial airliner capacity that sustains both local needs and a developing tourism industry. Many visitors have scuba or snorkelling in mind and arrive with pre-booked dive packages to stay at one of the island's four major resorts (two hotels and two condominiums). Other visitors – interested especially in nature tourism – can explore the 38 designated Heritage Sites & Trails, which feature helpful explanatory signs and panels. Alternative accommodation for the independent traveller includes bed & breakfast and over 20 guesthouses for short-term rental. As a diving destination, the Brac offers something unique. In 1996, a Russian naval frigate, renamed the MV Capt. Keith Tibbetts, was scuttled on the inside edge of the drop-off on the north-west coast. Today, well colonised with coral and other marine life, it is the only Russian-built warship in the Western hemisphere that divers can explore.

Cayman Brac

Hiking on the Bluff

Keith Tibbetts dive site

Christopher Columbus monument in Quincentennial Park

Pedal power!

New solar-powered lighthouse with replica of original

Cayman Brac Museum

Museum exhibit

Little Cayman
A unique experience

Point of Sand beach

The calm waters of the Caribbean

Although the smallest of the three islands, Little Cayman is one of the world's most reputed dive destinations. At the legendary Bloody Bay Wall Marine Park, on the northern shoreline, the sheer coral wall begins at 20 feet (9 metres) and plunges to a staggering 6,000 feet (1,829 m) and more. The park is also the scene of a historic anchorage: with deep water close to shore and a fresh-water source nearby, the bay once offered seafarers protection from prevailing winds.

Through the centuries many unlucky captains caught in storms have fouled their anchors in the reef and been forced to cut their lines. The anchors these mariners left behind may have meant disaster for them, but their misfortune has become a contemporary diver's delight. At least 12 anchors are embedded in the underwater wall, ranging from colonial wooden-stocked anchors to British Admiralty issue and iron-stocked schooner tackle.

This and other top dive sites continue to

Bloody Bay Wall, one of the world's most spectacular diving spots

Blossom Village

Coming ashore after a day's sailing

attract thousands of divers to Little Cayman. As a result, its reputation as a premier dive destination outshines almost everything else the tiny 10-mile long (16 kilometre) island has to offer.

Yet Little Cayman is about more than underwater adventures. Beginning with sun-blessed solitude and miles of untouched

A long-time resident

wilderness, it offers visitors a unique Caribbean experience. It has, for instance, over 40 designated 'heritage sites and trails', comprised of fascinating historical and cultural sites and woodland trails. Beachcombers should include tiny Owen Island (in the middle of South Hole Sound and accessible by kayak) and Point of Sand (on the south-east end) on their itineraries. They will often find themselves

alone on these glistening, enticing beaches. Those looking for light tackle action can challenge the bonefish, small tarpon and permit fish in the South Hole Sound. Or there is always the 15-acre (6 hectare) Tarpon Lake to visit, an inland brackish water pond that is home to a feisty species of tarpon.

With fewer than 100 full-time residents on the island, it is not surprising that birds and iguanas outnumber people by far. Home to the 203-acre (82 ha) Booby Pond Nature Reserve – the Cayman Islands' first RAMSAR wetland site – Little Cayman plays host to the largest known colony of Red-footed Boobies and the only breeding colony of Magnificent Frigate Birds in the Western Hemisphere.

Less visible than the island's winged creatures, the Sister Island Rock Iguana still enjoys preferential treatment from locals. Visitors never fail to delight in the 'Iguanas have the right of way' signs posted everywhere. Though there is an estimated population of 2,000 iguanas, spotting one can still be tricky, as they blend perfectly with their surroundings. A couple of regulars can, however, always be found sunbathing on the warm tarmac on Candle Lane close to the Lighthouse Point, and will gladly accept banana handouts from visitors.

A good way to get to this spot (and, in fact, to anywhere on the island) is to grab a bicycle. They are on offer free of charge at most resorts. Riders on the southern shore should look out for the Little Cayman Museum. Filled with local artefacts and old photographs, it offers a glimpse of the early years when the sale of coconuts and thatch rope drove the economy. Just to the west of the museum is Blossom Village, the 'commercial heart' of the island. It features the only grocery store, a bank (open two days weekly with no ATM), a car-rental agency, gasoline station and church.

The island might soon see some additional development. Plans are underway to replace the tiny airstrip with an airport and runway suitable for commercial airliners, similar to the one on neighbouring Cayman Brac. But for now, Little Cayman remains one of the Caribbean's best island hideaways and most visitors list the simple pleasure of soaking up solitude, while swinging in a hammock tied between two coconut trees, as the best reason to return.

The tranquil beauty of Owen Island

Booby Pond, a haven for many bird species

Grand Cayman wastewater treatment works

Serving the world's most popular drink

Desalination plant

The Water Authority of the Cayman Islands is a financially successful Government-owned statutory body. It has been responsible for the development of water and wastewater infrastructure as well as management of groundwater resources for the Cayman Islands since the enactment of the Water Authority Law in 1983.

Until just over 20 years ago, most people in the Cayman Islands relied on the collection of rainfall in cisterns and groundwater as sources of water for drinking and other uses. Problems with contaminated cisterns, contaminated groundwater and saline intrusion as well as rapid development led the Government to recognise the need for orderly and controlled development of potable water resources on the Islands.

In the 1960s, five freshwater 'lenses' (thin layers of water) were identified as large enough to be developed for a public water supply.

However, it was reported as early as 1975 that the thin freshwater lenses at West Bay and George Town had suffered through over-use and wastewater pollution, so they were not considered viable for commercial exploitation. In the mid-1970s, it was only along the main tourist resort area on West Bay Road that piped water was made available through a private company. In the early 1980s, with the surge in tourism and the construction of commercial and residential developments, there was an increased demand for a reliable source of clean, running water.

The Cayman Islands Government, understanding the infrastructure needs of the entire country, established the Water and Sewerage Project Office in 1981 with the mandate to establish a water and sanitation development plan for the Cayman Islands. With the enactment of the Water Authority Law in 1983, the Water Authority set in motion its

role as the country's 'Supplier of the World's Most Popular Drink'.

As it became clear that the early developments of fresh groundwater resources would not meet the needs of the rapid development happening in the country, the Water Authority embarked on an ambitious programme of infrastructure development. In those early days with a staff of five, and offices in a three-bedroom house, the Authority began its development with two large capital projects.

In 1986, work commenced on a multi-million dollar infrastructure project, the West Bay Beach Road wastewater collection system and wastewater treatment works. The George Town Piped Water Supply project commenced in early 1987. Both projects were commissioned and became operational in early 1988. By 1994, the piped water supply project had received several extensions and was completed up to the middle of Bodden Town by a private contractor. Since 1995, further extensions to the water distribution system have been and continue to be carried out by the Water Authority's own staff.

In Grand Cayman, the Authority supplies water to the district of George Town, Bodden Town,

East End and part of North Side, covering a total population of around 25,000 plus. The entire island of Grand Cayman will have access to piped water supplies by the end of 2007.

The Authority's customer base has more than doubled since 1996, from almost 5,000 service connections to over 10,000 in 2005. Correspondingly, from 1996 to 2005 water sales have doubled and staffing levels have almost tripled from 39 to 110 in 2006.

To provide service in the Sister Island of Cayman Brac, in 1991 the Authority commissioned a small piped water supply system there that now serves approximately 100 customers. For the Brac population not served through the pipelines, service is provided using Water Authority tanker trucks. There are no Water Authority-owned operations in Little Cayman, where there are a number of small desalination plants serving individual properties and developments.

Desalination by reverse osmosis is a relatively new, but very cost-effective application of an established scientific process. With continual advances in system and membrane design that boost efficiency and reliability, reverse osmosis will likely play a major role in freshwater production for years to come in the Cayman Islands.

The product water of the reverse osmosis process, as used by the Water Authority, removes more than 99.5% of the dissolved salts and is of a higher quality than the World Health Organisation guidelines for drinking water quality.

To meet expected water demand due to extension of the piped water services and the steadily increasing pace of development, the

Quality-control testing

Authority has to be proactive and install sufficient production and storage capacity to manage these needs. With a current installed water production capacity of 11,000 cubic metres per day in Grand Cayman and plans in place for an additional 4,000 cubic metres per day, the Authority is well able to cope with the peak dry-season demands. With water production capacity of 560 cubic metres per day in Cayman Brac, the Authority has sufficient water available to serve that island's needs.

Healthy, clean piped water to their door is a reality for more than 10,000 Water Authority customers. Furthermore, more than 90% of the Islands' residents have access to piped 'city water' through either Water Authority supplies

or those of the private company supplying all areas west of the capital George Town.

Another major activity of the Authority is the provision of sewerage services along the West Bay Beach Road. This area has the highest concentration of tourist activity. From here, domestic wastewater is collected through the Authority's sewer system and pumped to the wastewater treatment site in George Town.

The original wastewater treatment facility commissioned in 1988 consisted of four large, waste stabilisation ponds. However, because of the growth and development along West Bay Road area, this treatment facility has been replaced by a state-of-the-art sequencing batch reactor (SBR) wastewater treatment works, which will meet the island's needs for wastewater treatment in the long term. Additionally, the Authority is considering further treatment of the effluent produced at the wastewater treatment plant for use as irrigation water. The Authority sees water as too valuable a resource to put back into the ground, if re-use proves to be economically feasible.

The next step for the Water Authority is the extension of the current wastewater collection system. This will go into other areas, starting with the remaining ones adjacent to West Bay Road, George Town and West Bay.

The Water Authority maintains a quality control laboratory, which in 2002 received accreditation from the American Association for Laboratory Accreditation (A2LA). This made it the first Caribbean laboratory specialising in water and wastewater analyses to receive such recognition. After a natural hurricane disaster in 2004, the laboratory sustained some damage and subsequently requested that its accreditation status be categorised as "inactive" until the recovery was completed. The Authority expects to have the accreditation re-instated in 2005. In order to achieve and maintain accreditation, the laboratory undergoes a rigorous external review process that meets internationally recognised standards, thus assuring customers that the water sold by the Authority is wholesome. Under the Water Authority Law, the Authority is responsible for the management and protection of groundwater resources in the Cayman Islands. Priority is given to the protection and preservation of the fresh groundwater lenses. Grand Cayman has three major fresh groundwater lenses. These are located in East End, Lower Valley and North Side. Cayman Brac has a small fresh groundwater lens in the vicinity of Tibbetts Turn. There are no significant fresh groundwater lenses in Little Cayman. The only well field presently in operation by the

Control panels at the wastewater treatment works

Authority is in East End. Fresh groundwater is pumped from ten wells into a reservoir with 330 cubic metres capacity storage, from where it is sold to private trucking companies.

The Authority invests significantly in training and development of personnel. It supports many employees working towards university degrees or improves their basic skills through courses at local and overseas institutions.

Although the Authority is still investing extensively in capital infrastructure projects, it remains proud of its contribution to the local community. This is conducted through its support of sports and activities related to young people as well as other charitable organisations.

Over the last two decades, the Authority has continuously evaluated emerging technology and utilised sophisticated technology. They include the GPS (Global Positioning System) and GIS (Geographic Information Systems), which are used for tracking and mapping existing infrastructure and planning future infrastructure, and SCADA (Supervisory Control and Data Acquisition), used to obtain information from pumping stations, reservoirs and so on.

Cayman's rapid economic growth demands a high quality of service, which the Water Authority of the Cayman Islands is proudly able to deliver as the 'Supplier of the world's most popular drink'.

Enjoying the world's most popular drink

Health care

The Cayman Islands enjoy a high standard of general and specialist medical care. Overseen and regulated by the Ministry of Health Services, health care services are provided by the nation's Health Services Authority (HSA) and by the private sector.

The HSA operates all health care facilities previously run by the Government. These include a hospital in Grand Cayman, another in Cayman Brac, a public health unit, four District Health Centres, a General Practice Clinic at the Cayman Islands Hospital, dental and eye-care clinics, and a clinic in Little Cayman.

Since July 1997, all residents have been required to have minimum private-sector health insurance. This covers basic medical expenses, with the premium shared evenly between the employee and employer.

The nation's principal health care facility is the Cayman Islands Hospital in George Town, Grand Cayman. The 124-bed hospital – which was expanded in the late 1990s to include the modern, purpose-built Health Service Complex – provides accident and emergency services and a wide range of surgical services through its three operating theatres. Additional facilities include a

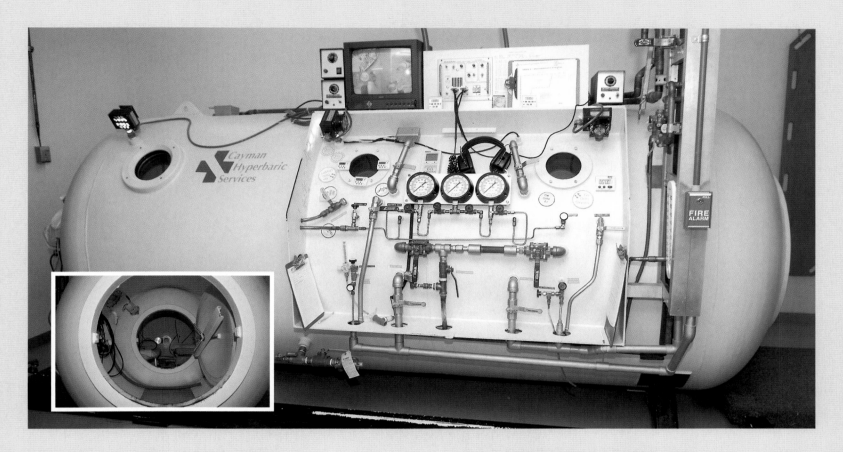

Critical Care Unit, pharmacy and laboratory services, and outpatient specialist clinics. The hospital has a dedicated staff of resident physicians and various visiting specialists from the United States and elsewhere.

The country also has a number of District Health Centres, which are located in Grand Cayman (West Bay, Bodden Town, North Side and East End) plus a clinic in Little Cayman. Each one is run by the Government through the Public Health Department.

Public health is the shared responsibility of the HSA and Government departments such as Environmental Health, Agriculture and the Mosquito Research & Control Unit. Programmes aimed at improving public health include immunisation, child health, genetics and nutrition.

In the Sister Islands, residents and visitors can turn for their health care needs to the Faith Hospital in Cayman Brac and the Little Cayman

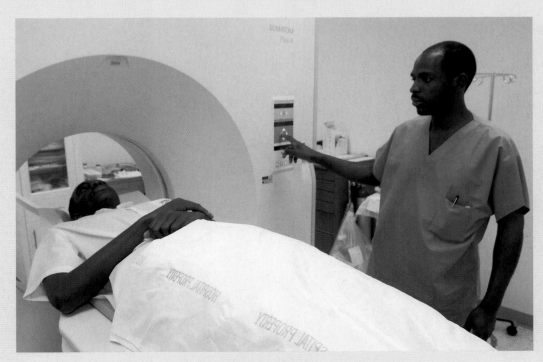

Clinic. The 18-bed hospital serves both islands and provides primary, basic secondary and emergency care. It features a modern inpatient unit, as well as an operating theatre, maternity, accident and emergency department, outpatient clinics and a public health department. In per capita terms, Faith Hospital has more physicians and speciality staff than any county hospital in the United States. However, acutely ill patients and those needing specialist care are transferred to the Cayman Islands Hospital in Grand Cayman.

The Little Cayman Clinic is a new purpose-built facility, complete with waiting and triage areas, a treatment room, doctors' office and a dental office. A resident nurse is on call around-the-clock.

As the Islands' population continues to grow and visitor numbers swell in the early 21st Century, their requirement for world-class health care services will surely grow. This is a challenge that the Government and its partners seem more than willing and able to meet.

A commitment to the future

By Nyda Flatley, B.A., M.Ed., Chief Education Officer, Cayman Islands Ministry of Education

The Cayman Islands Government Education system is based on the British system of education and offers universal primary and secondary education. There has been a comprehensive system of secondary education since the early 1970s.

Presently there are ten primary schools, two senior secondary schools, and one junior secondary (Middle) school. There is also one specialist school for students with mental or physical challenges and one alternative education centre for children with behavioural problems. The student population is over 4,000 in Government schools with over 400 teaching, administrative and specialist staff. As is done in the United Kingdom, the quality of teaching and learning is monitored by the Cayman Islands Schools' Inspectorate, which falls under the Ministry of Education.

Many features of the British system – such as Key Stage testing, and examinations such as GCSE and IGCSE – are retained in the Cayman Islands Government Education system. In order to contextualise our educational needs and acknowledge our geographical location in the Caribbean, however, it was decided in the late 1980s that our students would sit examinations set by the Caribbean Examinations Council (CXC). The syllabus content of the senior high schools on Cayman Brac and Grand Cayman, therefore, is largely dominated by the needs of the CXC examination with some input from the British examinations.

Significant curriculum development has occurred over the past 15 years, particularly in the core subjects of English, mathematics, social studies, and science. Following the dictates of the Education Law (1993 Review), religious education remains the only compulsory subject on the school curriculum. There is a vibrant visual and performing arts programme in

Cayman's future

most schools and the different arts areas are showcased in the Education Department's annual National Children's Festival of the Arts.

A new Education Bill is presently under review. Plans have also been made for the development of new secondary schools and major secondary school redevelopment in the coming years. Emphasis will be placed on technical and vocational education so as to meet the future development needs of the Islands' youth.

The Government system serves the needs of about two-thirds of the school age population. The educational needs of the remaining third are met by several private schools. These include the British-based Cayman Prep &

High School and St. Ignatius Catholic School, schools like Triple C School and Cayman International School which follow American programmes from Grades K-12, and schools like Wesleyan Christian Academy which follow an accelerated Christian education.

In January 2003, a series of integrated projects began in all schools, some of which were used to pilot the curriculum initiative entitled Improving Teaching, and Learning in the Cayman Islands (ITALIC) programme. Training of teachers was a first priority and the programme achieved its year-end goal of training over 250 teaching and administrative staff through the use of the Teacher Universe

Students at Cayman Prep and High School

Young musician at George Hicks High School

St. Matthew's University Medical School

Computer skills, an essential ingredient in today's competitive world

programme. Despite the setbacks of the hurricane in September 2004, much has been achieved with the training of mentor teachers for the Destination Maths and Destination Reading and the use of relevant software in schools.

There has been much growth in the area of communications and data management with the training of administrative and senior staff in the Star Student Information system. In the near future, student records will be accessed from a central server which will enable schools and the Education Department to communicate more effectively and efficiently. The server

Students at the University College of the Cayman Islands

University College Library

A positive teacher-student relationship

The friendly atmosphere at East End Primary School

will allow student information – such as attendance, academic records and registration – to be accessed easily and ensure more effective monitoring of trends in educational provision and performance.

It is impossible to speak of the Cayman Islands education system without referring to its amazing recovery and resilience after the hurricane of September 12, 2004. Only one of the ten schools on Grand Cayman was not damaged extensively. Roof repairs were needed in three primary schools, and both secondary schools, junior and senior, were significantly affected.

Radical methods were adopted to ensure that the educational needs of the Grand Cayman students were met after the storm. These included implementation of a shift system in the junior secondary section and provision made for Special Education needs students, examination students and pre-schools. A task force was also set up with staff from the Ministry of Education, the Education Department, and the Inspectorate. It concentrated not only on recovery and rebuilding of schools, but also on curriculum innovation and care of staff members.

As the Cayman Islands enters the 21st century, the focus for education is on a combination of quality teaching, curriculum development, technological advances, and innovative designs in our schools. These will enable us to meet the many challenges ahead and enhance the performance of our students, so that when they exit the system they will be fully prepared to contribute to a vibrant society.

188